Implementing, Managing, and Maintaining a Microsoft® Windows® Server 2003 Network Infrastructure

Project Lab Manual

Exam 70-291

Implementing, Managing, and Maintaining a Microsoft® Windows® Server 2003 Network Infrastructure

Project Lab Manual
Exam 70-291

First Edition

Kenneth C. Laudon, Series Designer
David Lundell, MCSE, MCT

The Azimuth Interactive MCSE/MCSA Team

Carol G. Traver, Series Editor
Kenneth Rosenblatt
Robin L. Pickering
Russell Polo
David Langley
Richard Watson, MCSE
Stacey McBrine, MCSE, MCSA
Tim Oliwiak, MCSE, MCT
Brien Posey, MCSE
Russell Jones, MCSE
Simon Sykes-Wright, MCSE
Nigel Kay, MCSE
Wale Soyinka, MCP
David W. Tschanz, MCSE
L. Ward Ulmer, MCSE, MCT
Mark Maxwell

PEARSON
Prentice
Hall

Upper Saddle River, New Jersey, 07458

Senior Vice President/Publisher: Natalie Anderson
Acquisitions Editor: Steven Elliot
Senior Marketing Manager: Steven Rutberg
Assistant Editor: Laura Burgess
Manager, Print Production: Christy Mahon
Production Editor & Buyer: Carol O'Rourke
Composition: Azimuth Interactive, Inc.
Quality Assurance: Digital Content Factory, Ltd.
Cover Printer: Phoenix Color
Printer/Binder: Courier, Bookmart Press

10 9 8 7 6 5 4 3 2 1
ISBN 0-13-145603-2

To our families,
for their love, patience,
and inspiration.

Brief Contents

Contents

The purpose of this Project Lab Manual is to provide you, the student, with another opportunity to review Windows Server 2003 concepts and skills, and to apply them to situations that you are likely to encounter on the job. The Prentice Hall Certification Series textbooks contain a great deal of conceptual and hands-on material. The Prentice Hall Certification Series Project Lab Manuals are designed to give you an opportunity to put those concepts and skills to work in a variety of different real-world on-the-job situations, and to understand the textbook contents in greater depth.

The Project Lab Manuals are organized in the same two-page highly illustrated format with conceptual material and instructions on the left-hand page, and screenshots and conceptual diagrams on the right-hand page. The Lessons in the Project Lab Manuals follow the Lessons in the textbook. Each Project Lab Manual Lesson is composed of a number of projects that reinforce the concepts and skills taught in the accompanying textbooks.

Project Lab Manual Lesson Contents

The Project Lab Manual Lessons have a number of elements designed to speed your learning and help you understand key concepts and skills.

Introductory Page: Each Lesson begins with an introductory page that reviews the key concepts and skills that you will be asked to apply in the lesson.

Scenario: Each Lesson has a brief scenario that describes the setting in which the projects take place. These scenarios provide you with a sense of how the concepts and skills that you have learned in the book are used in realistic business settings.

Project/Objective Table: Each Lesson includes a table that lists the Lesson projects and the corresponding exam objective supported. Where the project relates to a basic understanding of the subject matter, this is referred to as "Basic knowledge." You will always know how a project relates to MCSE/MCSA exam requirements.

General Requirements: At the beginning of each Lesson, there is a description of the hardware and software that you will need to complete the projects in the Lesson.

Project's Exam Objective: For each project there is a description of the specific MCSA/MCSE exam objective supported by the project.

Overview: Each project presents a specific assignment that builds on the Lesson's main scenario.

Learning Objective: Each project includes a specific learning objective that describes what you will be able to do after completing the project.

Specific Requirements: A list of specific requirements for each project is provided.

Estimated Completion Time: For each project, there is an estimated time for completion based on the experience of MCSE/MCSA professionals and instructors in colleges and training institutes. You should use these estimates only as a guide because your actual completion times will depend on your prior experience with Windows Server 2003.

Project Steps: Each project includes a set of step-by-step instructions for completing the project. These instructions are similar to those in the main textbook, but often differ because new options and pathways may be explored in the Project Lab Manuals.

Tips: Throughout the Project Lab Manuals you will find Tips and Cautions that offer you suggestions or comments about completing the project and working with Windows Server 2003.

Graphics and Illustrations: As you can expect from the Prentice Hall Certification Series, there are many screenshots and conceptual graphics provided that show you how the software should look at various points in the project. These are intended to familiarize you with the Windows Server 2003 environment and assure you that you are on the right track.

Quality Assurance

We have made every effort to ensure that the Project Lab Manuals are written to the same quality standards as the main textbook and the Interactive Solution CD-ROM. The Project Lab Manuals are written by MCSE and MCSA professionals with many years of real-world experience. The initial instructions and scenarios are then reviewed by independent technical editors who test each project, and each step. These results are then verified by the MCSE/MCSA team at Azimuth and the Series Designer and Editor. The end result is a product that students and instructors can understand and trust.

Notice

The projects in the Project Lab Manuals have been built using the most recent release of Windows Server 2003, Windows 2000 Server, and Windows XP Professional software. Your school or other institution may be using an earlier release of the software, or its environment may differ in some respects from the environment in which the projects were built. At times, these variations in environment and service packs can cause variations in the progression of steps and screenshots so that a screenshot in the book does not precisely match the screen you may be looking at. If this should occur, please report this to the authors at the Web site for this book.

1

Introducing Microsoft Windows Server 2003 Network Infrastructure

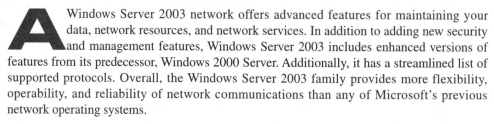

A Windows Server 2003 network offers advanced features for maintaining your data, network resources, and network services. In addition to adding new security and management features, Windows Server 2003 includes enhanced versions of features from its predecessor, Windows 2000 Server. Additionally, it has a streamlined list of supported protocols. Overall, the Windows Server 2003 family provides more flexibility, operability, and reliability of network communications than any of Microsoft's previous network operating systems.

Windows Server 2003's network infrastructure consists of computers, devices, and the services through which the computers in a network communicate with each other. Before creating a network infrastructure, you need to develop a plan to use the features of Windows Server 2003 effectively. Network planning involves four phases: analysis, design, testing, and deployment.

To facilitate communication among the computers in your Windows Server 2003 network, the following supported protocols can be used:

◆ Transmission Control Protocol/Internet Protocol (TCP/IP)
◆ NWLink
◆ AppleTalk
◆ Infrared Data Association (IrDA)

Note that the NetBEUI protocol is not supported in Windows Server 2003, nor is the DLC protocol.

Additionally, Windows Server 2003 provides various networking services for the network. These include:

◆ Dynamic Host Configuration Protocol (DHCP)
◆ Domain Name System (DNS)
◆ Windows Internet Naming Service (WINS)
◆ Routing and Remote Access Service (RRAS)
◆ Network Address Translation (NAT)
◆ Security Services
◆ Microsoft Certificate Services

This lesson includes projects that will help you become more familiar with the steps involved in setting up a Windows Server 2003, the protocols and services required in a network infrastructure, and Windows Server 2003's security services and features.

Scenario

You are the network administrator for a small company. Your company is planning to move to a new location and will be installing a new computer network based on Windows Server 2003 technology. Management has asked you to provide an overview of the steps involved in implementing the new network infrastructure.

Lesson 1 Introducing Microsoft Windows Server 2003 Network Infrastructure	
Project	**Exam 70-291 Objective**
1.1 Identifying the Phases in Setting Up a Windows Server 2003 Network	Basic knowledge
1.2 Identifying Protocols and Services Required in a Network Infrastructure	Basic knowledge
1.3 Identifying Security Features to Implement	Basic knowledge

General Requirements

There are no special requirements for this lesson. However, you may find it helpful to refer to Lesson 1 in your Prentice Hall Certification Series Exam 70-291 textbook for further information about the topics covered by the projects in this lesson.

project 1.1	*Identifying the Phases in Setting Up a Windows Server 2003 Network*
exam objective	Basic knowledge
overview	To provide the information requested by management, you have decided to create a presentation on the process of setting up a Windows Server 2003 network **(Figure 1-1)**.
learning objective	After completing this project, you will be more familiar with the main steps involved in setting up a Windows Server 2003 network.
specific requirements	None
estimated completion time	20 minutes
project steps	Prepare a presentation that lists and explains the main steps involved in setting up a Windows Server 2003 network.

Figure 1-1 Phases in Setting up a Windows Server 2003 Network

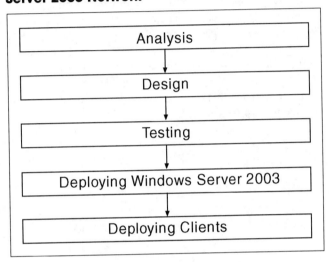

project 1.2

Identifying Protocols and Services Required in a Network Infrastructure

exam objective

Basic knowledge

overview

Your company's new network will be based on the TCP/IP protocol suite. The network will contain computers running different operating systems such as Windows 2000 Server, Windows 2000 Professional, Novell NetWare, and Mac OS. All the computers will be connected to the Internet. As the network administrator, you need to ensure that data can be exchanged between these computers. To do so, you need to identify the right protocols to be used. You also need to identify the services that will be required for IP address allocation and to translate domain names to IP addresses. Create a presentation on the protocols and the services that will be used (**Table 1-1** and **Figure 1-2**).

learning objective

After completing this project, you will more familiar with the protocols and services required in a network infrastructure.

specific requirements

None

estimated completion time

20 minutes

project steps

1. Identify and describe the advantages, disadvantages, and recommended uses of the protocol required for communication between the Windows Server 2003 and the Novell NetWare computers.
2. Identify and describe the advantages, disadvantages, and recommended uses of the protocol required for communication between the Windows Server 2003 and the Apple Macintosh computers.
3. Identify and describe the service used for the dynamic allocation of IP addresses.
4. Identify and describe the service used on the Internet to locate IP-based computers by translating their host names (domain names) to their associated IP addresses.

Table 1-1   Advantages and Disadvantages of the Protocols Supported by Windows Server 2003

Protocol	Advantages	Disadvantages	Recommended Usage
TCP/IP	• Native protocol for Unix, Novell, and Windows networks • Not vendor specific • Flexible		Large environments that support Internet applications
NWLink	• Routable protocol • Easy-to-configure		Connection with NetWare resources
AppleTalk	• Inexpensive • Supports Apple's LocalTalk cabling scheme, as well as Ethernet and IBM token ring.	Requires specific AppleTalk hardware and software.	Connection with Macintosh computers and printers
IrDA	• Provides wireless, walk-up, line-of-sight connectivity between devices. • Easy-to-use	• Complex to install because wireless devices require IrDA ports for networking. • Line-of-sight requirement can pose logistical problems.	Wireless, point-to-point networking
PPTP	• Secures connections with encryption. • Works over a variety of network types.		Connection to corporate networks over the Internet
L2TP	• Works over a variety of network types. • Compresses message headers.	Does not encrypt data.	Virtual private networks

Figure 1-2 Windows Server 2003 services

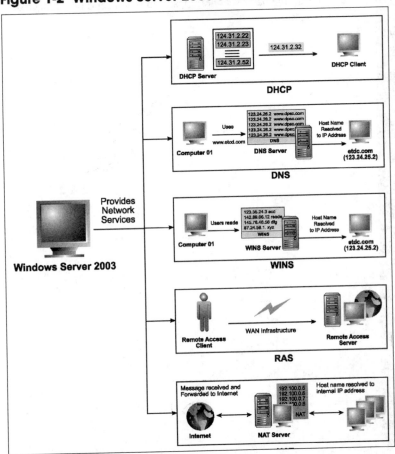

project 1.3

Identifying Security Features to Implement

exam objective

Basic knowledge

overview

Your company is subject to regulations that require that only specific users with the proper authority have access to certain records. These records should be encrypted to help prevent unauthorized access. Based on the previous exercise, in which all the computers will be connected to the Internet, create an appendix to your protocols and services presentation that lists Windows Server 2003 security features (**Figure 1-3**) and explains which features should be implemented to achieve this result.

learning objective

After completing this project, you will be more familiar with the security services and features to consider when designing a Windows Server 2003 network.

specific requirements

None

estimated completion time

20 minutes

project steps

1. Identify and describe the service that will be used to authenticate users and prevent unauthorized access to certain records.
2. Identify and describe the tools that should be installed to administer these services.
3. Explain the basic technologies used when sending encrypted data and to ensure a secure transaction.

Figure 1-3 Windows Server 2003 security services

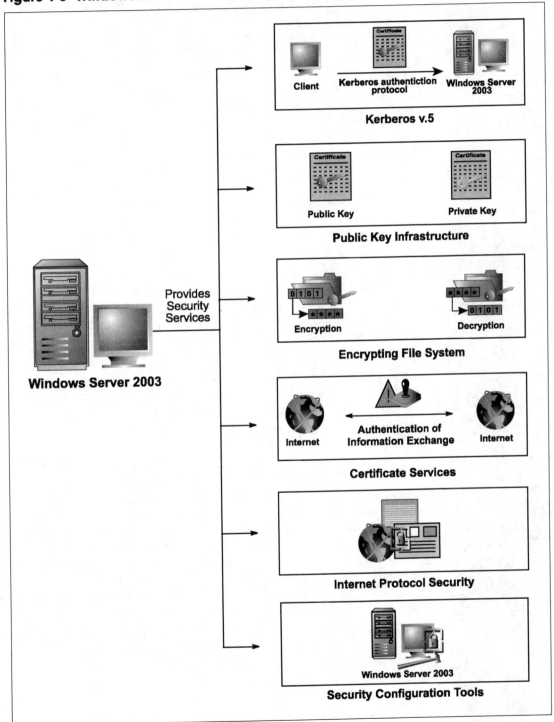

2

Understanding IP Addressing and TCP/IP

The Windows Server 2003 Transmission Control Protocol/Internet Protocol (TCP/IP) suite is a set of protocols (or rules) that facilitates communication among resources of varying configurations across a network. These rules manage the content, format, timing, sequencing, and error control of the messages that are exchanged by devices on a network. Overall, the protocol determines how clients and servers must package data in order to send it to other computers on the network, as well as how they should interpret data that they receive.

Each network resource that communicates through TCP/IP is identified with a unique IP address. An IP address is a 32-bit number assigned to the hosts on the network. Computers, printers, routers, and other devices that are identified with an IP address are all hosts. Each IP address consists of a network ID and a host ID. The network ID identifies the network to which the host belongs, and the host ID identifies the destination or source host on the network.

Before you implement TCP/IP on a network, you should take some time to plan the implementation. You must consider such factors as the network's size, as well as its physical and logical layout. After planning, the first step in assigning an IP address to a host on a network is to make sure that TCP/IP has been installed on the host. Then, you need to configure TCP/IP by assigning addresses to the hosts, which can be done manually or dynamically. Once you have assigned addresses to the hosts on the network, different kinds of traffic can begin to flow into the network.

Verification of TCP/IP configuration ensures that your computer can connect to other TCP/IP hosts on the network. Troubleshooting TCP/IP problems can occupy a large portion of a network administrator's time. Diagnostic utilities such as Ping and Ipconfig enable you to troubleshoot problems associated with TCP/IP. The Ping utility verifies that one host can reach another across the network. If you cannot ping another host, error messages may reveal routing or other problems. Receiving no response to the Ping utility can even reveal information about network problems. The Ipconfig utility provides information about configuration, IP address, subnet mask, and default gateway of the host computer.

This lesson contains projects that will enable you to practice confirming that TCP/IP has been installed, manually installing and configuring TCP/IP, and testing and troubleshooting the TCP/IP configurations on a Windows Server 2003 system. You will also become familiar with how Automatic Private IP Addressing (APIPA) works.

Scenario

You are working as a network administrator for a company that manufactures floor-polishing equipment. You have been asked to add new server computers to an existing network. You need to configure these servers and assign them IP addresses to enable them to communicate within the network. You must also be prepared to troubleshoot any problems that occur during the deployment of these servers to the network.

Lesson 2 Understanding IP Addressing and TCP/IP

Project	Exam 70-291 Objective
2.1 Confirming Installation of TCP/IP	Configure TCP/IP addressing on a server computer.
2.2 Manually Configuring TCP/IP	Configure TCP/IP addressing on a server computer.
2.3 Testing the TCP/IP Configuration	Configure TCP/IP addressing on a server computer.
2.4 Using Automatic Private Addressing (APIPA)	Diagnose and resolve issues related to Automatic Private IP Addressing (APIPA).
2.5 Disabling Automatic Private Addressing (APIPA)	Diagnose and resolve issues related to Automatic Private IP Addressing (APIPA).
2.6 Using Netsh to Reset All TCP/IP Settings	Troubleshoot TCP/IP addressing.

General Requirements

To complete the projects in this lesson, you will need administrative rights on a Windows 2003 Server computer connected to the network. You may also find it helpful to refer to Lesson 2 in your Prentice Hall Certification Series Exam 70-291 textbook for further information about the topics covered by the projects in this lesson.

project 2.1

Confirming Installation of TCP/IP

exam objective

Configure TCP/IP addressing on a server computer.

overview

Confirm that TCP/IP is installed on the Windows Server 2003 computer.

learning objective

After completing this project, you will know how to confirm that TCP/IP has been installed and how to manually install TCP/IP (if it was removed somehow) on a Windows Server 2003 computer.

specific requirements

See general requirements.

estimated completion time

20 minutes

project steps

Confirm TCP/IP is installed

1. Click **Start** on the taskbar, point to **Control Panel**, point to **Network Connections**, right-click **Local Area Connection**, then click **Properties** on the shortcut menu (**Figure 2-1**). This will open the **Local Area Connection Properties** dialog box.
2. If **Internet Protocol (TCP/IP)** is listed, it is already installed.
3. Click **Internet Protocol (TCP/IP)**.
4. Notice that the **Uninstall** button is grayed out (**Figure 2-2**).

If TCP/IP is not installed for some reason, install it

5. Click **Install** to open the **Select Network Component Type** dialog box.
6. Click **Protocol** in the **Click the type of network component you want to install** list box (**Figure 2-3**).
7. Click **Add** to open the **Select Network Protocol** dialog box.
8. Select the **Internet Protocol (TCP/IP)** option and click **OK**.
9. After the command completes, close the **Local Area Connections Properties** dialog box.

tip

TCP/IP is installed by default with Windows Server 2003 and cannot be uninstalled.

caution

For exceptions, see Microsoft Knowledge Base articles 325356 and 318584.

Figure 2-1 Accessing the Local Area Connection Properties dialog box

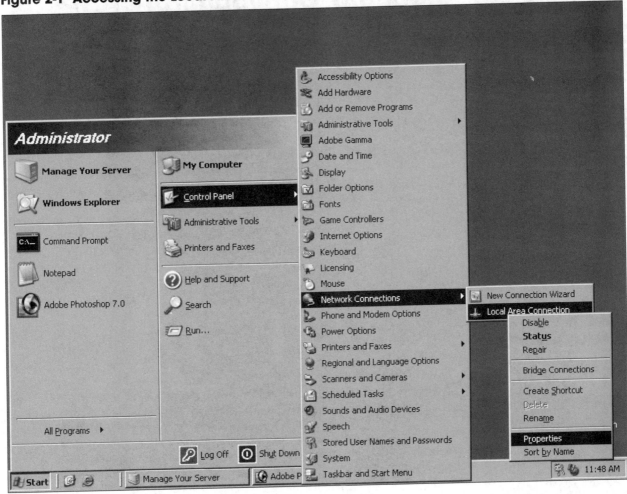

**Figure 2-2 Local Area Connection
Properties dialog box — TCP/IP installed**

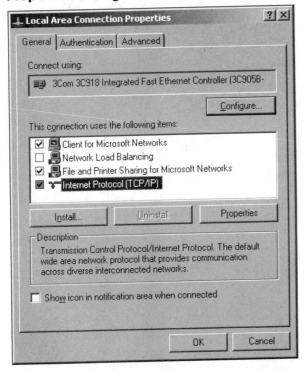

**Figure 2-3 Select Network
Component Type dialog box**

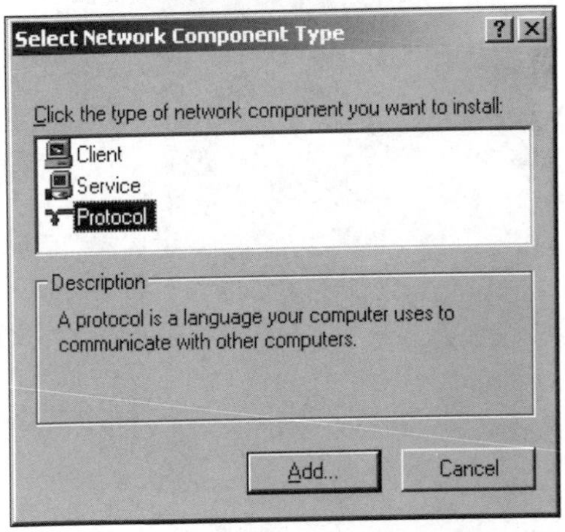

project 2.2

Manually Configuring TCP/IP

exam objective

Configure TCP/IP addressing on a server computer.

overview

After confirming that TCP/IP is installed, you need to configure TCP/IP for IP addresses. Since you are not adding very many new computers to the network, you have decided to configure TCP/IP manually on these new computers.

learning objective

After completing this project, you will know how to manually configure TCP/IP on a Windows Server 2003 computer.

specific requirements

To complete this project, you must have completed Project 2.1.

estimated completion time

10 minutes

project steps

1. Open the **Local Area Connection Properties** dialog box.
2. On the **General** tab, select the **Internet Protocol (TCP/IP)** option in the **This connection uses the following items** list box **(Figure 2-4)** and then click the **Properties** button. This will display the **Internet Protocol (TCP/IP) Properties** dialog box.
3. Select the **Use the following IP address** option button and type in the IP address, subnet mask, and default gateway (if applicable) in their respective fields.
4. You may type in the IP address of the preferred DNS server for manual configuration and, if applicable, the IP address of an alternate DNS server. The **Use the following DNS server addresses** option button has already been selected for you when you selected the **Use the following IP address** option in the **Internet Protocol (TCP/IP) Properties** dialog box **(Figure 2-5)**.
5. Click **OK** to close the dialog box.

caution

While configuring, you should not add arbitrary IP addresses to your network. An incorrect IP address can cause serious problems for your network administrators.

Figure 2-4 Selecting Internet Protocol (TCP/IP)

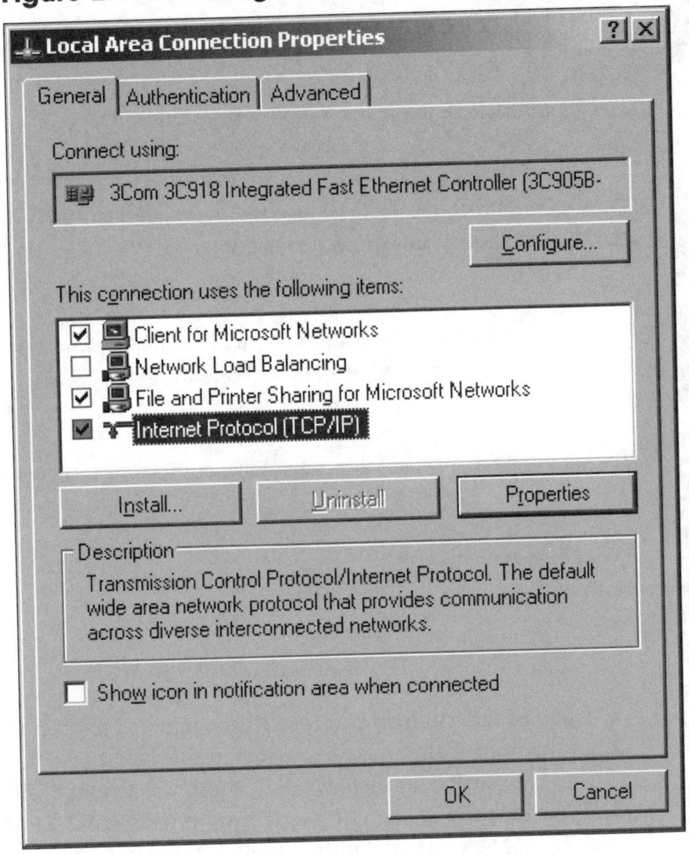

Figure 2-5 Configuring an IP address

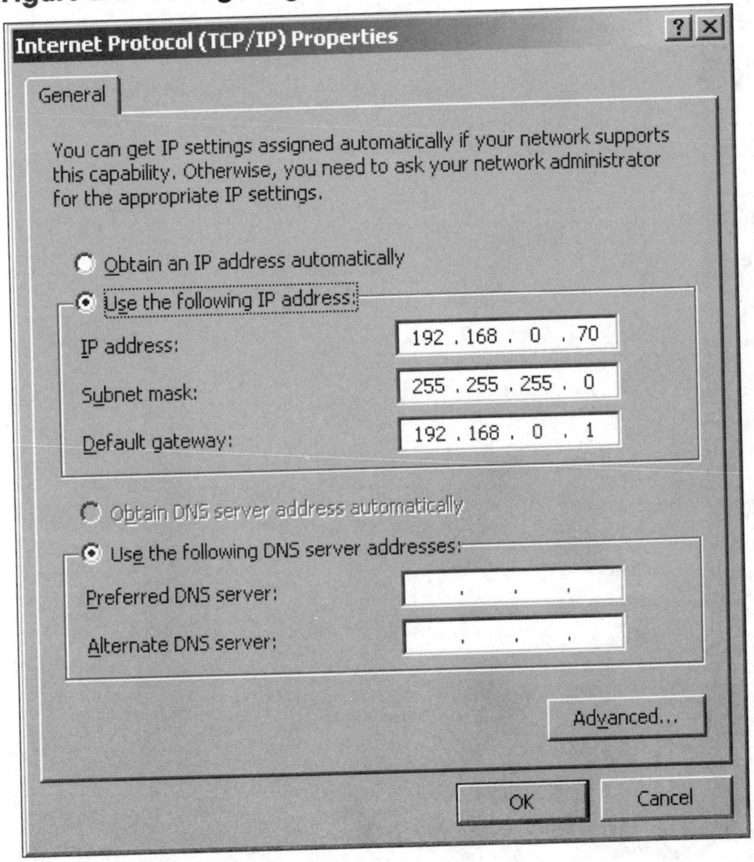

project 2.3

Testing the TCP/IP Configuration

exam objective	Configure TCP/IP addressing on a server computer.
overview	After configuring the TCP/IP protocol, you need to verify your IP settings to make sure that the new computer can connect to the other TCP/IP hosts on the network.
learning objective	After you have completed this project, you will know how to test the TCP/IP protocol configurations on a Windows Server 2003 system.
specific requirements	To complete this project, you must have completed Projects 2.1 and 2.2.
estimated completion time	10 minutes

project steps

1. Click **Start**, and then click the **Run** command to open the **Run** dialog box.
2. In the **Run** dialog box, type **cmd** in the **Open** text box (**Figure 2-6**) and click **OK** or press [**Enter**]. This displays the **Command Prompt** window.
3. Type **ipconfig** at the command prompt (**Figure 2-7**) and press [**Enter**]. This displays TCP/IP configuration information such as the IP address, subnet mask, and default gateway (**Figure 2-8**).
4. Type **ping <IP address>** at the command prompt. Press [**Enter**]. The statistics on data transfer between the two hosts are displayed on the screen (**Figure 2-9**).
5. Close the **Command Prompt** window.

Figure 2-6 Using the Run dialog box to open the Command Prompt window

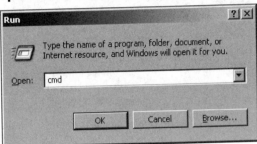

Figure 2-7 The Ipconfig command

Figure 2-8 Using Ipconfig to test TCP/IP configuration

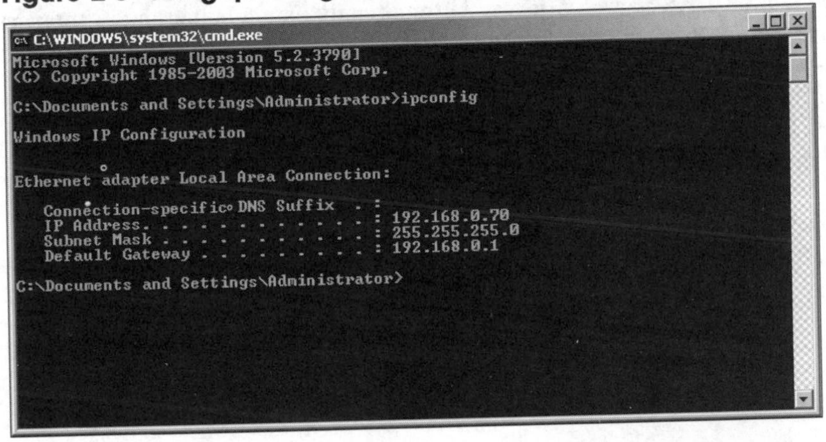

Figure 2-9 Reply messages received through the Ping utility

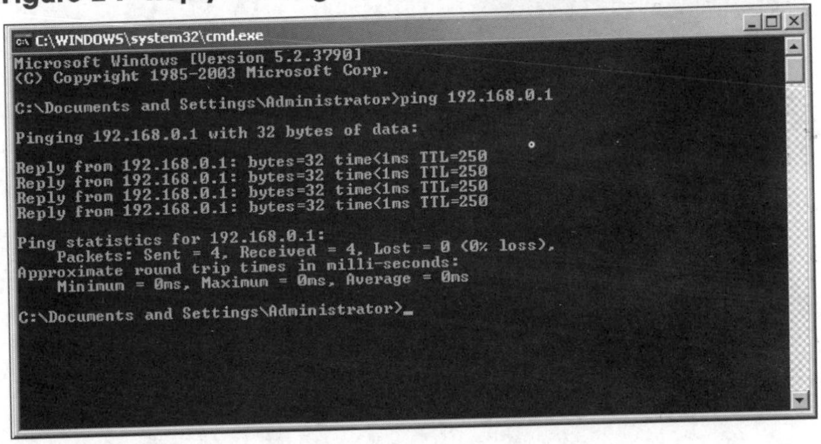

project 2.4

Using Automatic Private IP Addressing (APIPA)

exam objective

Diagnose and resolve issues related to Automatic Private IP Addressing (APIPA).

overview

Later, you will set up a DHCP server and client computers that use a DHCP server to automatically configure IP addresses. You need to understand what will happen to computers that are set up to use DHCP when there is no DHCP server available. In this case, they will use APIPA.

learning objective

After you have completed this project, you will be more familiar with how APIPA works on a Windows Server 2003 system.

specific requirements

To complete this project, you must have completed project 2.1 and be on a network where DHCP is turned off or otherwise unavailable.

estimated completion time

30 minutes

project steps

1. Open the **Local Area Connection Properties** dialog box.
2. On the **General** tab, select the **Internet Protocol (TCP/IP)** option in the **This connection uses the following items** list box and then click the **Properties** button. This will display the **Internet Protocol (TCP/IP) Properties** dialog box.
3. Select the **Obtain an IP address Automatically** option button.
4. Select the **Obtain DNS Server Address Automatically** option button in the **Internet Protocol (TCP/IP) Properties** dialog box (**Figure 2-10**).
5. Click **OK** to close the dialog box.
6. Redo Project 2.3. Observe that there is no default gateway and the IP address is between 169.254.0.1 and 169.254.255.254 and that the subnet mask is 255.255.0.0. Further observe that you cannot ping any other computer on the network unless it is also using APIPA.
7. Redo Project 2.2 to configure a static IP address.

Figure 2-10 Obtaining an IP address and DNS server address automatically

Internet Protocol (TCP/IP) Properties

General | Alternate Configuration

You can get IP settings assigned automatically if your network supports this capability. Otherwise, you need to ask your network administrator for the appropriate IP settings.

- ⦿ Obtain an IP address automatically
- ○ Use the following IP address:

  IP address:

  Subnet mask:

  Default gateway:

- ⦿ Obtain DNS server address automatically
- ○ Use the following DNS server addresses:

  Preferred DNS server:

  Alternate DNS server:

Advanced...

OK   Cancel

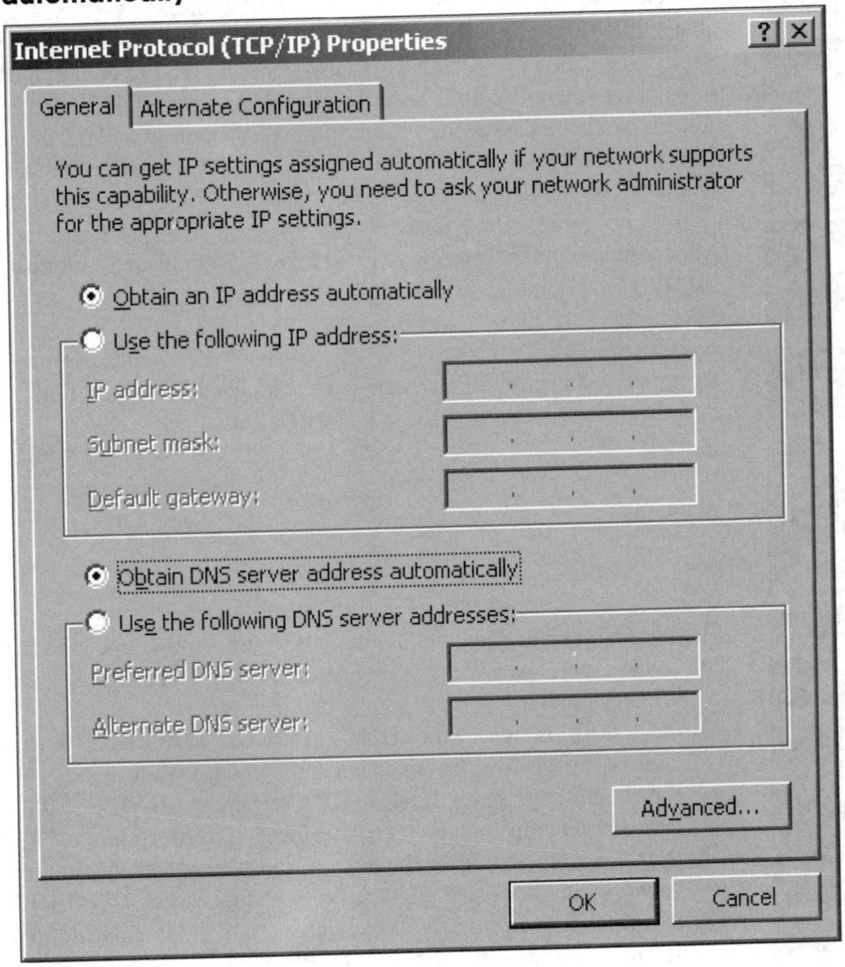

project 2.5

Disabling Automatic Private IP Addressing (APIPA)

exam objective

Diagnose and resolve issues related to Automatic Private IP Addressing (APIPA).

overview

Allowing computers to assign themselves IP addresses with APIPA may seem like a good alternative when a DHCP server is not available, but it can also cause problems, especially for large organizations whose networks use DNS and require communication across networks. If a computer that normally receives its IP address from a DHCP server assigns itself an APIPA address when the DHCP server fails, the APIPA address will remain in effect when the DHCP server resumes functionality. This will leave the computer isolated from the network and unable to communicate. One solution to this possible problem is to disable APIPA.

learning objective

After completing this project, you will know how to disable Automatic Private IP Addressing (APIPA) on a Windows Server 2003 computer.

specific requirements

To complete this project, you must have completed Projects 2.1 and 2.2.

estimated completion time

10 minutes

project steps

1. Click **Start** and then click **Run** on the Start menu to open the **Run** dialog box.
2. In the **Open** text box, type **regedt32 (Figure 2-11)** and click **OK**. The **Registry Editor** window opens.
3. Click the plus sign next to **HKEY_LOCAL_MACHINE** to expand the node in the left pane of the window. Continue expanding nodes **(Figure 2-12)** until you have browsed to the following key: **HKEY_LOCAL_MACHINE\SYSTEM\CurrentControlSet \Services \Tcpip\Parameters\Interfaces\<adaptername> (Figure 2-13)**.
4. Right-click the name of the network adapter (a hexadecimal value that refers to your network interface card), point to **New**, and then click **DWORD Value**.
5. Rename the new DWORD Value, which is highlighted in the right pane, **IPAutoconfigurationEnabled (Figure 2-14)**.
6. Double-click the new DWORD Value to open the **Edit DWORD Value** dialog box and make sure that the **Value data** text box is set to **0 (Figure 2-9)**. The **Hexadecimal** option button should be selected in the **Base** section by default. Click **OK**.
7. Close the Registry Editor.

tip

In Windows Server 2003, regedt32 and regedit open the same tool, which has replaced both the tools shipped with Windows 2000.

Figure 2-11 Using the Run dialog box to open the Registry Editor

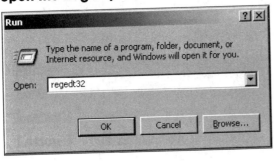

Figure 2-12 HKEY_LOCAL_MACHINE node partially expanded

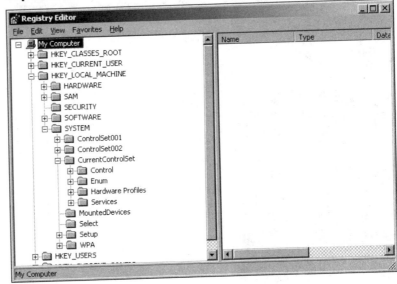

Figure 2-13 Adapter name keys in HKEY_LOCAL_MACHINE

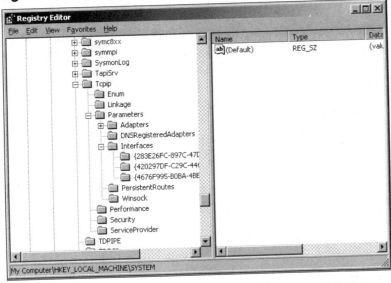

Figure 2-14 Creating a new DWORD value

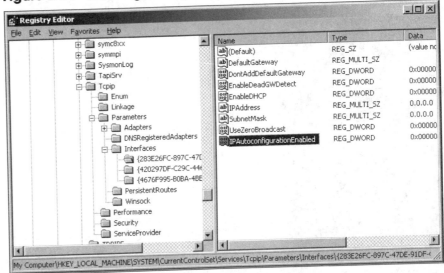

project 2.6

Using Netsh to Reset all TCP/IP Settings

exam objective

Troubleshoot TCP/IP addressing.

overview

One possible way to troubleshoot TCP/IP problems is to reset TCP/IP to all of its defaults. In earlier versions this was done by uninstalling and reinstalling the TCP/IP protocol stack. Since this is not normally possible under Windows Server 2003, you use the **netsh interface ip reset** command to reset all TCP/IP properties to their defaults.

learning objective

After you have completed this project, you will know how to use the Netsh interface ip reset command to reset all TCP/IP properties to their defaults.

specific requirements

See general requirements.

estimated completion time

10 minutes

project steps

1. Click **Start** and then click **Run** to open the **Run** dialog box.
2. In the **Run** dialog box, type **cmd** in the **Open** text box and press **[Enter]**. This displays the **Command Prompt** window.
3. Type **netsh interface ip reset c:\IPResetLog.txt** in the Command Prompt window (**Figure 2-15**) and press **[Enter]**.
4. Type **notepad c:\IPResetLog.txt** in the Command Prompt window and press **[Enter]**.
5. Note that the command has gone through and reset all Registry keys associated with TCP/IP.

Figure 2-15 The netsh interface ip reset command

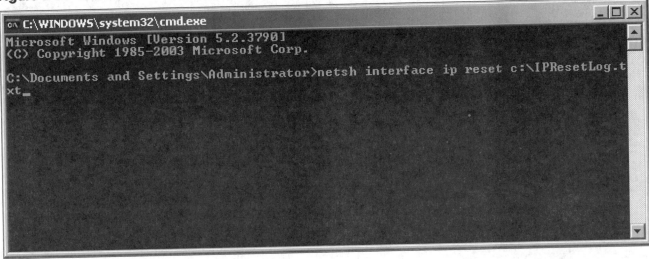

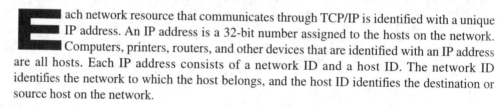

LESSON

3

Understanding IP Routing

Each network resource that communicates through TCP/IP is identified with a unique IP address. An IP address is a 32-bit number assigned to the hosts on the network. Computers, printers, routers, and other devices that are identified with an IP address are all hosts. Each IP address consists of a network ID and a host ID. The network ID identifies the network to which the host belongs, and the host ID identifies the destination or source host on the network.

Routing refers to the process of selecting the path by which a source computer transfers packets of data across networks to a destination computer. When a host has to send data to another host, it uses the Internet Protocol (IP) address of the destination host to identify where to send the information. A source host can only send data to a computer on its own LAN segment. If the destination is on another LAN segment or another network, the source host sends its packet (which includes the IP address of the destination as well as the IP address of the source) to a router on its own LAN. The router then will deliver the packet to its destination, or continue to forward the packet until it reaches a router that can deliver it.

A host can transmit data directly to another computer on the same network. However, if the destination computer resides on a different network, a router, or gateway, acts as the interface between the two networks. When a packet arrives at a gateway, the network adapter sends the IP datagram to be inspected at the IP layer. IP reads the destination address on the packet and then looks for the address in a routing table. The router then forwards the packet on the appropriate path to the network based on the network's entry in the routing table. A router helps minimize communication costs and maximize communication efficiency by determining the best path for the packet to follow to the intended destination. Windows Server 2003 computers store defined routes in routing tables automatically.

Demand-dial routing is a Windows Server 2003 feature that enables a server to detect when an alternative to the network path is required for a connection. For example, to connect to a low-traffic remote network, you might use dial-up telephone lines instead of leased dedicated lines. The server uses a dial-up connection to forward packets across a Point-to-Point Protocol (PPP) link, establishing a temporary link between the server and the destination path.

This lesson contains projects that will let you practice manually updating a routing table, enabling and configuring Routing and Remote Access Service, configuring a static route, creating a dial-on-demand route, and using the Arp, Route print, Tracert, and Pathping commands to troubleshoot network problems.

Scenario

You are working as the network administrator for Heavenly Chill Inc., a refrigeration equipment supplier. There have been some changes made to your company's network, and as a result you need to make changes in the network router's routing table. You also want to implement a low-cost plan to provide an alternate connection if your network's dedicated lease line fails. To do this, you will implement demand-dial routing in your network. You are also going to be deploying a server to the Internet and want to limit the protocols that can be used to connect to it.

Lesson 3 Understanding IP Routing

Project	Exam 70-291 Objective
3.1 Updating a Routing Table Manually	Manage TCP/IP routing. Manage routing tables. Troubleshoot connectivity to the Internet.
3.2 Enabling Routing and Remote Access Service	Manage routing protocols. Manage Routing and Remote Access routing interfaces.
3.3 Configuring Static Routing	Manage TCP/IP routing.
3.4 Installing and Configuring Demand-dial Routing	Manage routing protocols. Manage Routing and Remote Access routing interfaces. Troubleshoot demand-dial routing.
3.5 Troubleshooting IP Routing Problems	Manage TCP/IP routing.
3.6 Configuring IP Packet Filters	Manage routing ports. Manage packet filters. Manage Routing and Remote Access routing interfaces.

General Requirements

To complete the projects in this lesson, you will need administrative rights on a Windows Server 2003 computer connected to the network. You may also find it helpful to refer to Lesson 3 in your Prentice Hall Certification Series Exam 70-291 textbook for further information about the topics covered by the projects in this lesson.

project 3.1

Updating a Routing Table Manually

exam objective

Manage TCP/IP routing. Manage routing tables. Troubleshoot connectivity to the Internet.

overview

Heavenly Chill's network has just been upgraded, and as a result, you decide to manually add routes to the routing table of the network's router.

learning objective

After completing this project, you will know how to update a routing table manually on a Windows Server 2003 computer.

specific requirements

See general requirements. You will also need to have an IP address on the 192.168.0.0/24 network.

estimated completion time

10 minutes

project steps

1. Click **Start** and then click **Run** to open the **Run** dialog box.
2. In the **Open** text box, type **cmd**, and then click **OK**. The **Command Prompt** window opens.
3. At the command prompt, type **route add 135.50.2.0 mask 255.255.255.0 192.168.0.1**. This command enables communication with the host 135.50.2.0 from a gateway host 192.168.0.1.
4. Press the **[Enter]** key to update the routing table manually with the new route.
5. Type **route print** at the command prompt and press **[Enter]** to view the new route added to the routing table (**Figure 3-1**).
6. Close the Command Prompt window.

tip

For the gateway, you will need to use an IP address on your local subnet.

caution

The route added here will disappear upon rebooting. To add a persistent route use the route -p option.

Figure 3-1 IPv4 Route Table

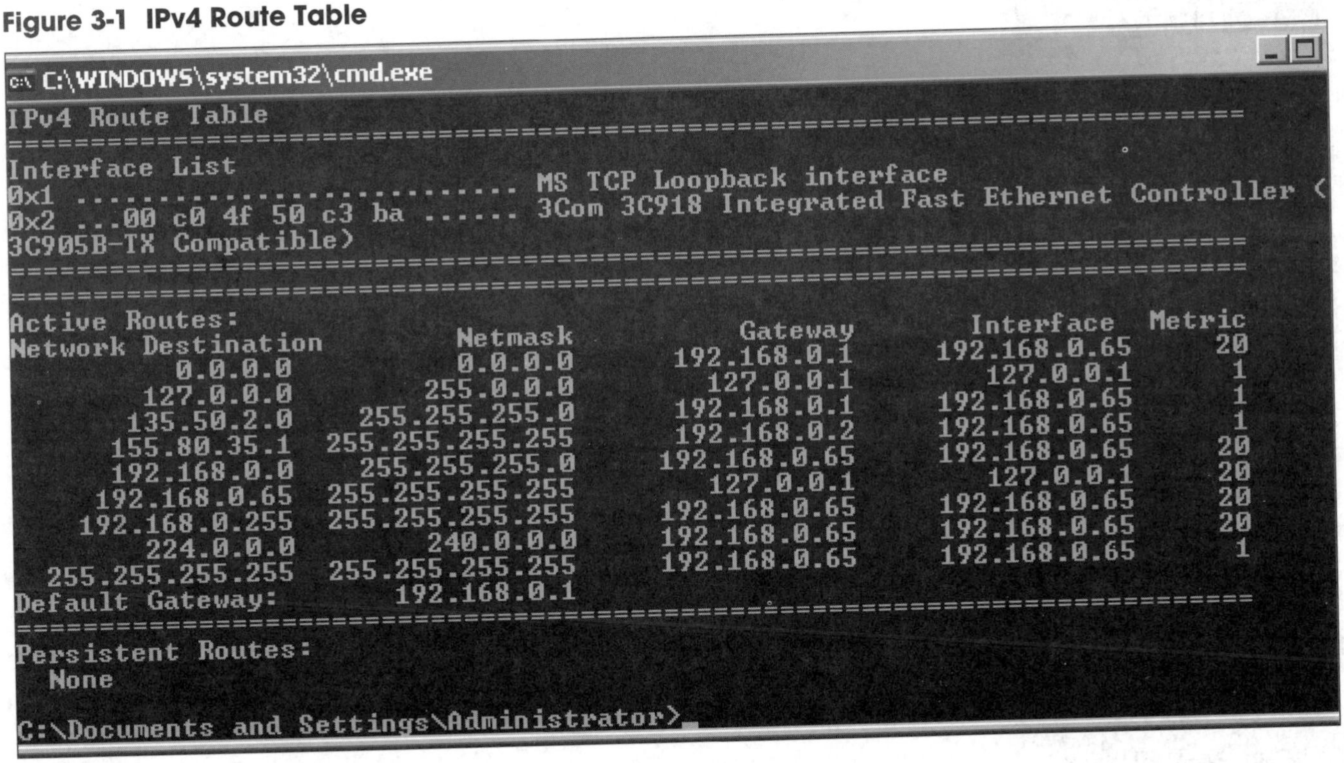

```
 C:\WINDOWS\system32\cmd.exe                                             _ □ ✕

IPv4 Route Table
===========================================================================
Interface List
0x1 ...........................  MS TCP Loopback interface
0x2 ...00 c0 4f 50 c3 ba ......  3Com 3C918 Integrated Fast Ethernet Controller (
3C905B-TX Compatible)
===========================================================================
===========================================================================
Active Routes:
Network Destination        Netmask          Gateway       Interface  Metric
        0.0.0.0          0.0.0.0      192.168.0.1    192.168.0.65     20
      127.0.0.0        255.0.0.0        127.0.0.1        127.0.0.1      1
     135.50.2.0    255.255.255.0      192.168.0.1    192.168.0.65      1
    155.80.35.1  255.255.255.255      192.168.0.2    192.168.0.65      1
    192.168.0.0    255.255.255.0     192.168.0.65    192.168.0.65     20
   192.168.0.65  255.255.255.255        127.0.0.1        127.0.0.1     20
  192.168.0.255  255.255.255.255     192.168.0.65    192.168.0.65     20
      224.0.0.0        240.0.0.0     192.168.0.65    192.168.0.65      1
255.255.255.255  255.255.255.255     192.168.0.65    192.168.0.65
Default Gateway:       192.168.0.1
===========================================================================
Persistent Routes:
  None

C:\Documents and Settings\Administrator>
```

project 3.2

Enabling Routing and Remote Access Service

exam objective

Manage routing protocols. Manage Routing and Remote Access routing interfaces.

overview

A new network has been created for Heavenly Chill's Marketing division. You need to connect this new network to Heavenly Chill's existing network. Before you can configure static routes and demand-dial routing, you must enable Routing and Remote Access Service on the server.

learning objective

After completing this project, you will be know how to enable and configure Routing and Remote Access Service on a Windows Server 2003 computer.

specific requirements

See general requirements.

estimated completion time

10 minutes

project steps

1. Log on to the computer as an **Administrator**.
2. Click **Start**, point to **Administrative Tools**, and then click **Routing and Remote Access** to open the **Routing and Remote Access** console.
3. Right-click the server icon in the tree in the left pane of the console window and select **Configure and Enable Routing and Remote Access (Figure 3-2)** on the shortcut menu.
4. The **Routing and Remote Access Server Setup Wizard** appears. Click **Next**.
5. The **Configurations** screen appears. Click the **Custom configuration** option button **(Figure 3-3)** and click **Next**.
6. The **Custom Configuration** screen appears. Place a check mark in the **LAN routing** check box **(Figure 3-4)**. Do not select any other services. Then click **Next**.
7. The **Completing the Routing and Remote Access Server Setup Wizard** screen appears. Click **Finish** to complete the setup of Routing and Remote Access Service.
8. When prompted, click **Yes** to start the **Routing and Remote Access Service**.
9. Close the Routing and Remote Access console.

Figure 3-2 Enabling Routing and Remote Access

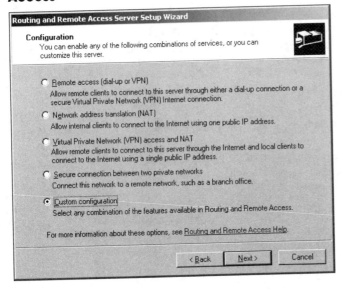

Routing and Remote Access

File   Action   View   Help

Routing and Remote Access
  Server Status
  DLTEST

DLTEST (local)

Configure and Enable Routing and Remote Access

Disable Routing and Remote Access

All Tasks

View

Delete
Refresh

Properties

Help

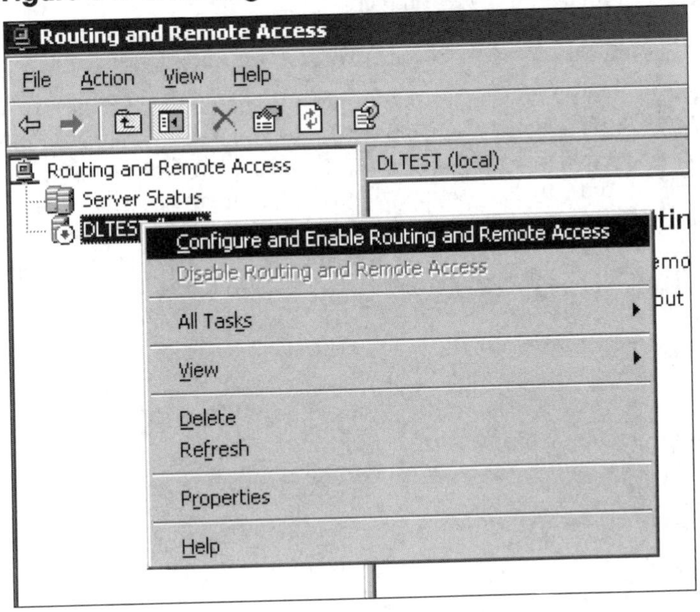

Figure 3-3 Configuring Routing and Remote Access

Routing and Remote Access Server Setup Wizard

Configuration
You can enable any of the following combinations of services, or you can customize this server.

○ Remote access (dial-up or VPN)
  Allow remote clients to connect to this server through either a dial-up connection or a secure Virtual Private Network (VPN) Internet connection.

○ Network address translation (NAT)
  Allow internal clients to connect to the Internet using one public IP address.

○ Virtual Private Network (VPN) access and NAT
  Allow remote clients to connect to this server through the Internet and local clients to connect to the Internet using a single public IP address.

○ Secure connection between two private networks
  Connect this network to a remote network, such as a branch office.

● Custom configuration
  Select any combination of the features available in Routing and Remote Access.

For more information about these options, see Routing and Remote Access Help.

< Back   Next >   Cancel

Figure 3-4 Custom Configuration of Routing and Remote Access

Routing and Remote Access Server Setup Wizard

Custom Configuration
When this wizard closes, you can configure the selected services in the Routing and Remote Access console.

Select the services that you want to enable on this server.

☐ VPN access

☐ Dial-up access

☐ Demand-dial connections (used for branch office routing)

☐ NAT and basic firewall

☑ LAN routing

< Back   Next >   Cancel

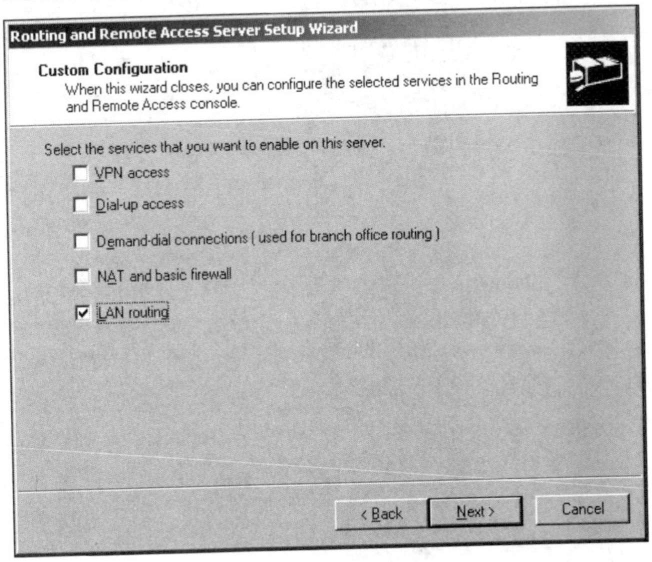

project 3.3

Configuring Static Routing

exam objective

Manage TCP/IP routing.

overview

Due to security requirements, communication to host **155.80.35.0** (which contains the confidential CAD drawings of Chill's next generation refrigeration equipment) has to pass through a special firewall that does not handle most traffic and is not the default gateway. In order to do this, you will need to configure a static route.

learning objective

After completing this project, you will know how to configure a static route on a Windows Server 2003 network.

specific requirements

To complete this project, you must have completed project 3.2.

estimated completion time

10 minutes

project steps

1. Open the **Routing and Remote Access** console.
2. Click the plus sign next to your server's name in the left pane of the console window to expand the server node.
3. Click **IP Routing** in the left pane of the console window to see the options for IP Routing in the details pane on the right side of the console window.
4. Right-click **Static Routes** in the details pane (**Figure 3-5**), and then click **New Static Route** on the shortcut menu to add a new static route. The **Static Route** dialog box opens.
5. Click the down arrow button next to the **Interface** list box to view the interface options.
6. Click **Local Area Connection** on the Interface list to add a new network to the LAN.
7. Type **155.80.35.0** in the **Destination** box to specify the destination for the route.
8. Type **255.255.255.0** in the **Network mask** box to specify the network mask for the static route.
9. Type the router IP address, **198.186.0.2**, in the **Gateway** box to specify the forwarding IP address for the static route.
10. Type the metric associated with the static route in the **Metric** spin box. The default value is **1** (**Figure 3-6**).
11. Click **OK** to complete the configuration of the new static route.
12. Close the Routing and Remote Access console window.

tip

For the gateway you will need to use an IP address on your local subnet.

Figure 3-5 New Static Route command

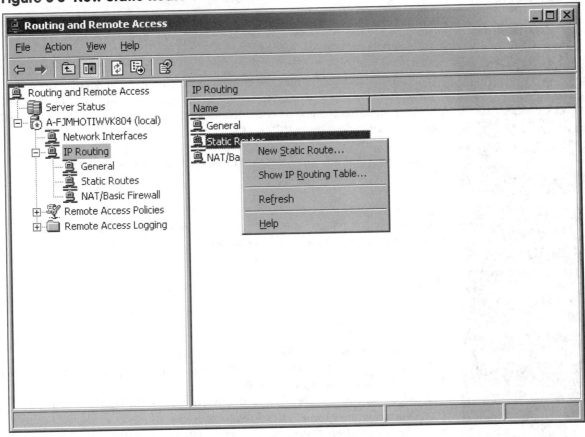

Figure 3-6 Static Route dialog box

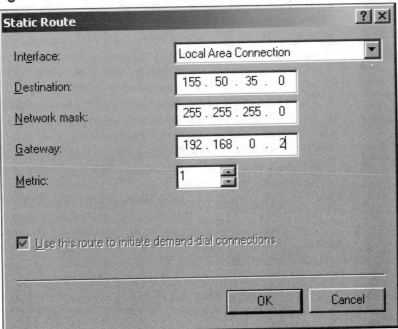

project 3.4

Installing and Configuring Demand-dial Routing

exam objective

Manage routing protocols. Manage Routing and Remote Access routing interfaces. Troubleshoot demand-dial routing.

overview

Heavenly Chill needs to securely communicate with their coolant supplier. The supplier, We're Very Cool, does not want to have a bank of modems to allow dial in. Additionally, your budget is tight. Therefore, you cannot afford a private circuit. Consequently, you will need to configure a dial-on demand VPN route.

learning objective

After completing this project, you will know how to create a dial-on-demand route on a Windows Server 2003 system.

specific requirements

To complete this project, you must have completed project 3.2 and be on a network where DHCP is turned off or otherwise unavailable.

estimated completion time

30 minutes

project steps

1. Open the **Routing and Remote Access** console.
2. If necessary, click the plus sign next to your server's name in the left pane of the console window to expand the server node.
3. Right-click your server's name in the left pane of the console window to display the context sensitive menu. Click **Properties**.
4. The **Properties** dialog box appears. On the **General** tab, click the **LAN and demand-dial routing** option button (**Figure 3-7**) and then click **OK**.
5. When prompted to restart the router, click **Yes** (**Figure 3-8**).
6. Right-click **Network Interfaces** in the left pane of the console window, and then click **New Demand-dial Interface** on the shortcut menu (**Figure 3-9**).
7. The **Demand-dial Interface Wizard** appears. Click **Next** to advance to the **Interface Name** screen.
8. Replace the default name (**Figure 3-10**) in the **Interface name** text box with an new name that is more descriptive. Click **Next** to open the **Connection Type** screen.
9. Click the **Connect using virtual private networking (VPN)** option button. Click **Next** to open to the **VPN Type** screen (**Figure 3-11**).
10. Leave the **Automatic selection** option button selected and click **Next**.
11. The **Destination Address** screen appears. Type the destination host's name or IP address in the **Host name or IP address** text box. Click **Next**.
12. The **Protocols and Security** screen opens. Make sure that the **Route IP packets on this interface** check box is selected and click **Next** to advance to the **Static Routes for Remote Networks** screen.
13. Click **Add** to open the **Static Route** dialog box. In the appropriate boxes, enter the address, network mask, and metric of the remote network with which this connection will communicate. Then, click **OK** to confirm the new static route.
14. Click **Next** to advance to the **Dial Out Credentials** screen. Type a **user name** and the **domain** name in the **User name** and **Domain** text boxes, respectively. Type a password in the **Password** text box, and then type the same password in the **Confirm password** text box (**Figure 3-11**). Click **Next**.
15. Click **Finish** to complete the Demand-dial Interface Wizard.

tip

This route won't actually work for you unless there is a VPN server whose address you know and for whom you have legitimate credentials.

Figure 3-7 Routing and Remote Access Server Properties

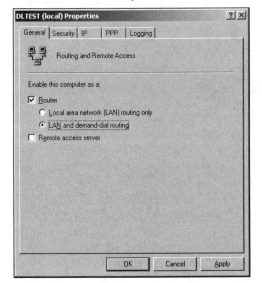

Figure 3-8 Restart the Router message box

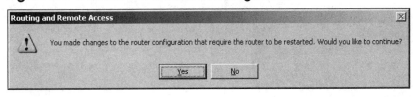

Figure 3-9 New Demand-dial interface command

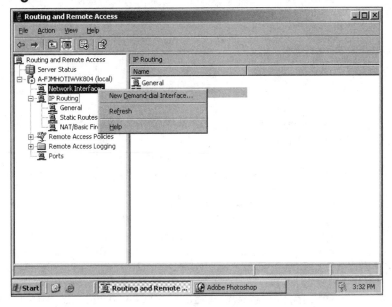

Figure 3-10 Default name for demand-dial interface

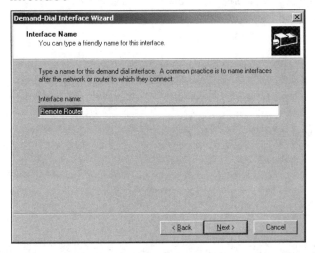

Figure 3-11 VPN Type screen

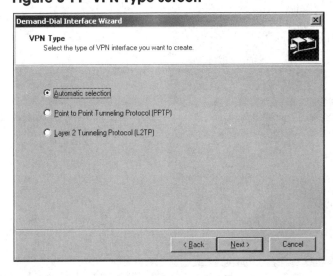

project 3.5

Troubleshooting IP Routing Problems

exam objective

Manage TCP/IP routing.

overview

When routing problems occur on the network it will be helpful to use some of the common TCP/IP commands provided by Windows Server 2003 to troubleshoot the failure.

learning objective

After you have completed this project, you will know how to use some common TCP/IP commands provided by Windows Server 2003 for troubleshooting network problems:

◆ Arp -a: List the Address Resolution cache.
◆ Route print: Lists the current routing table.
◆ Tracert: Verify the path and metrics network traffic uses to reach a destination host.
◆ Pathping: Determine network path and reports packet loss information of the various hops taken to reach the final destination.

specific requirements

See general requirements.

estimated completion time

10 minutes

project steps

1. Click **Start**, and then click the **Run** command. This will display the **Run** dialog box.
2. In the **Open** text box, type **cmd**, and then click **OK**.
3. At the command prompt, type **arp -a**.
4. Press the **[Enter]** key. This will display the ARP cache on the server (**Figure 3-12**).
5. At the command prompt, type **route print**.
6. Press the **[Enter]** key. This will display the current routing table (Note the new manual route added in Project 3.1) (**Figure 3-13**).
7. Type **tracert www.azimuth-interactive.com** at the command prompt and press **[Enter]**. Each hop to a router is recorded along with the time it took to reach the router, the FQDN (fully-qualified DNS host name) of the router, and the IP address of the router (**Figure 3-14**).
8. Type **pathping www.azimuth-interactive.com** and press **[Enter]**. Pathping sends an ICMP echo request message to each router on the path from your computer to the destination host. The path of router hops is recorded as it is when you use Tracert. Then, Pathping calculates the percentage of packets lost out of packets sent (**Figure 3-15**).
9. Close the Command Prompt window.

Figure 3-12 Viewing the contents of the Arp cache

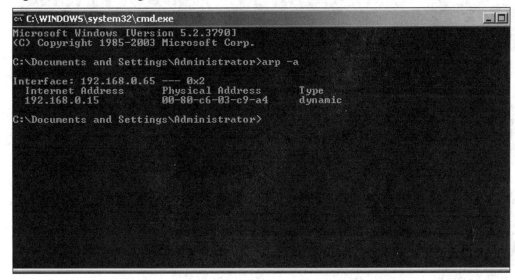

```
C:\WINDOWS\system32\cmd.exe                                        _ □

Microsoft Windows [Version 5.2.3790]
(C) Copyright 1985-2003 Microsoft Corp.

C:\Documents and Settings\Administrator>arp -a

Interface: 192.168.0.65 --- 0x2
  Internet Address      Physical Address      Type
  192.168.0.15          00-80-c6-03-c9-a4     dynamic

C:\Documents and Settings\Administrator>
```

Figure 3-13 Using Route print to display the local routing table

```
C:\WINDOWS\system32\cmd.exe                                        _ □

===========================================================================
Interface List
0x1 ........................... MS TCP Loopback interface
0x2 ...00 c0 4f 50 c3 ba ...... 3Com 3C918 Integrated Fast Ethernet Controller (
3C905B-TX Compatible)
===========================================================================
===========================================================================
Active Routes:
Network Destination        Netmask          Gateway       Interface  Metric
          0.0.0.0          0.0.0.0      192.168.0.1    192.168.0.65     20
        127.0.0.0        255.0.0.0        127.0.0.1      127.0.0.1      1
       135.50.2.0    255.255.255.0      192.168.0.1    192.168.0.65      1
      155.50.35.0    255.255.255.0      192.168.0.2    192.168.0.65      1
      155.80.35.1  255.255.255.255      192.168.0.2    192.168.0.65      1
      192.168.0.0    255.255.255.0     192.168.0.65    192.168.0.65     20
     192.168.0.65  255.255.255.255        127.0.0.1      127.0.0.1     20
    192.168.0.255  255.255.255.255     192.168.0.65    192.168.0.65     20
        224.0.0.0        240.0.0.0     192.168.0.65    192.168.0.65     20
  255.255.255.255  255.255.255.255     192.168.0.65    192.168.0.65      1
Default Gateway:        192.168.0.1
===========================================================================
Persistent Routes:
  None

C:\Documents and Settings\Administrator>
```

Figure 3-14 Results of the Tracert command

```
C:\WINDOWS\system32\cmd.exe                          _ ᵇ ×
Microsoft Windows [Version 5.2.3790]
(C) Copyright 1985-2003 Microsoft Corp.

C:\Documents and Settings\Administrator>tracert www.azimuth-interactive.com

Tracing route to azimuth-interactive.com [64.49.254.91]
over a maximum of 30 hops:

  1    <1 ms    <1 ms    <1 ms  192.168.0.1
  2    13 ms    11 ms    10 ms  10.135.0.1
  3     8 ms     9 ms     7 ms  dstswr1-vlan2.rh.osngny.cv.net [67.83.231.33]
  4     8 ms     9 ms     8 ms  67.83.231.1
  5     9 ms     8 ms     8 ms  r1-srp1-0.cr.whplny.cv.net [65.19.120.17]
  6     9 ms     8 ms    10 ms  r1-srp5-0.wan.whplny.cv.net [65.19.120.1]
  7    11 ms    10 ms    11 ms  r1-srp0-0.in.nycmny83.cv.net [65.19.96.83]
  8    17 ms    18 ms    17 ms  r1-pos1-0.in.asbnva16.cv.net [167.206.8.150]
  9    15 ms    16 ms    17 ms  as6128-gw.asbn.tutelecom.net [65.19.100.89]
 10    15 ms    16 ms    17 ms  66.192.255.228
 11    32 ms    33 ms    34 ms  core-02-so-0-0-0-0.atln.tutelecom.net [66.192.
5.23]
 12    65 ms    63 ms    65 ms  dist-02-so-0-0-0-0.snan.tutelecom.net [168.215
3.109]
 13    63 ms    63 ms    65 ms  hagg-01-ge-1-3-0-0.snan.tutelecom.net [64.132.
8.254]
 14    68 ms    67 ms    65 ms  64.132.228.26
 15    67 ms    68 ms    67 ms  vl130.core1.sat.rackspace.com [64.39.2.33]
 16    68 ms    68 ms    68 ms  vl905.aggr5.sat2.rackspace.com [64.39.2.82]
 17    67 ms    68 ms    69 ms  64.49.254.91

Trace complete.

C:\Documents and Settings\Administrator>
```

Figure 3-15 Using the Pathping command

```
C:\WINDOWS\system32\cmd.exe                          _ ᵇ ×
C:\Documents and Settings\Administrator>pathping www.azimuth-interactive.com

Tracing route to azimuth-interactive.com [64.49.254.91]
over a maximum of 30 hops:
  0  a-fjmhotiwvk804 [192.168.0.65]
  1  192.168.0.1
  2    *  10.135.0.1
  3  dstswr1-vlan2.rh.osngny.cv.net [67.83.231.33]
  4  67.83.231.1
  5  r1-srp1-0.cr.whplny.cv.net [65.19.120.17]
  6  r1-srp5-0.wan.whplny.cv.net [65.19.120.1]
  7  r1-srp0-0.in.nycmny83.cv.net [65.19.96.83]
  8  r1-pos1-0.in.asbnva16.cv.net [167.206.8.150]
  9  as6128-gw.asbn.tutelecom.net [65.19.100.89]
 10  66.192.255.228
 11  core-02-so-0-0-0-0.atln.tutelecom.net [66.192.255.23]
 12  dist-02-so-0-0-0-0.snan.tutelecom.net [168.215.53.109]
 13  hagg-01-ge-1-3-0-0.snan.tutelecom.net [64.132.228.254]
 14  64.132.228.26
 15  vl130.core1.sat.rackspace.com [64.39.2.33]
 16  vl905.aggr5.sat2.rackspace.com [64.39.2.82]
 17  64.49.254.91

Computing statistics for 425 seconds...
            Source to Here   This Node/Link
Hop  RTT    Lost/Sent = Pct  Lost/Sent = Pct  Address
  0                                            a-fjmhotiwvk804 [192.168.0.65]
                               0/ 100 =  0%    |
  1    2ms   0/ 100 =  0%     0/ 100 =  0%     192.168.0.1
                               0/ 100 =  0%    |
  2   36ms   0/ 100 =  0%     0/ 100 =  0%     10.135.0.1
                               0/ 100 =  0%    |
  3   10ms   0/ 100 =  0%     0/ 100 =  0%     dstswr1-vlan2.rh.osngny.cv.net
.83.231.33]
```

project 3.6

Configuring IP Packet Filters

exam objective

Manage routing ports. Manage packet filters. Manage Routing and Remote Access routing interfaces.

overview

In order to conserve bandwidth and improve security, you will configure filters that will limit the traffic that can pass through your server to the network. IP filtering enables you to establish secure connections based on the source, destination, and type of traffic.

learning objective

After you have completed this project, you will know how to configure IP packet filters.

specific requirements

See general requirements.

estimated completion time

15 minutes

project steps

1. Click **Start**, point to **Control Panel**, point to **Network Connections**, and then click **Local Area Connection**.
2. In the **Local Area Connection Status** dialog box, click **Properties** to open the **Local Area Connection Properties** dialog box.
3. On the **General** tab, highlight **Internet Protocol (TCP/IP)** in the **This connection uses the following items** list box.
4. Click **Properties** to open the **Internet Protocol (TCP/IP) Properties** dialog box.
5. Click **Advanced** to open the **Advanced TCP/IP Settings** dialog box.
6. Click the **Options** tab, select **TCP/IP Filtering** in the **Optional settings** list box, and then click **Properties**. The **TCP/IP Filtering** dialog box opens.
7. Click the **Enable TCP/IP Filtering (all adapters)** check box.
8. Click the first **Permit Only** option button, which enables the **Add** and **Remove** buttons under the **TCP Ports** section (**Figure 3-16**).
9. Click **Add** to open the **Add Filter** dialog box.
10. Type **80** in the **TCP Port** field to enable the TCP port for HTTP traffic only (**Figure 3-17**).
11. Click **OK** to close the Add Filter dialog box. The value 80 appears in the TCP Ports section (**Figure 3-18**). You can similarly enable filtering for the UDP and IP ports.
12. Add several filters from the list shown in **Table 3-1**.
13. Close all open dialog boxes.

Figure 3-16 The TCP/IP Filtering dialog box

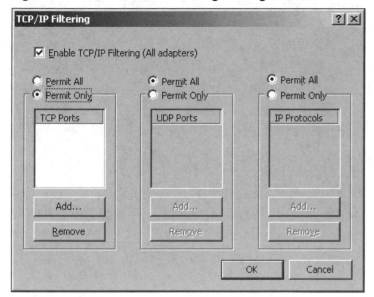

Figure 3-17 The Add Filter dialog box

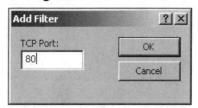

Figure 3-18 Allowing only HTTP traffic through the TCP port

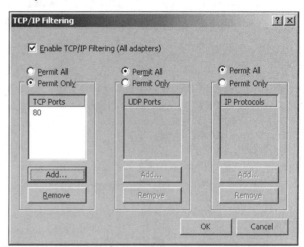

Table 3-1 Common port numbers used for filtering		
Port Type	**Port Number**	**Function**
Common TCP Port Numbers	20	FTP Server data channel
	21	FTP Server control channel
	23	Telnet
	53	DNS name queries
	80	HTTP service
	110	Post Office Protocol 3 (POP3)
	119	Network News Transfer Protocol (NNTP)
	139	NetBIOS Session service
	137	NetBIOS Name Server (NBNS)
	389	LDAP
	443	Secure HTTP (HTTPS)
	1723	Point-to-Point Tunneling Protocol (PPT)
	3389	Remote Desktop Protocol (RDP)
Common UDP Port Numbers	161	Simple Network Management Protocol (SNMP)
	520	Routing Information Protocol (RIP)
	1701	Layer 2 Tunneling Protocol (L2TP)
Common IP Protocol Numbers	1	Internet Control Message (ICMP)
	2	Internet Group Management (IGMP)
	6	TCP
	17	UDP
	47	Generic Routing Encapsulation (GRE)
	50	IPSec Encapsulating Security Payload (ESP)
	51	IPSec Authentication Header (AH)

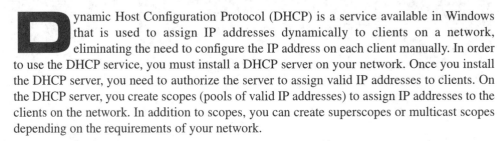

Implementing and Managing DHCP

Dynamic Host Configuration Protocol (DHCP) is a service available in Windows that is used to assign IP addresses dynamically to clients on a network, eliminating the need to configure the IP address on each client manually. In order to use the DHCP service, you must install a DHCP server on your network. Once you install the DHCP server, you need to authorize the server to assign valid IP addresses to clients. On the DHCP server, you create scopes (pools of valid IP addresses) to assign IP addresses to the clients on the network. In addition to scopes, you can create superscopes or multicast scopes depending on the requirements of your network.

When the IP addresses of clients are updated dynamically, the DNS service must be notified so that it can update the client name-to-IP address and IP address-to-name mapping on the DNS server. On a Windows Server 2003 network, you can integrate a DHCP server with the DNS service to enable dynamic updates of the DNS service.

Once you have installed and configured the DHCP Server service, you need to administer the DHCP server by performing tasks such as starting, stopping, and resuming the DHCP Server service, and performing DHCP database maintenance. Additionally, you need to monitor the DHCP server's performance and troubleshoot it for problems that might occur on your network. If you are working with a large network, you may also find it useful to install the DHCP Relay Agent protocol to enable your DHCP clients to request IP addresses from a DHCP server that is located on a remote subnet.

This lesson contains projects that will enable you to practice installing and authorizing a DHCP server; creating and managing DHCP scopes, including creating a superscope; integrating DHCP with DNS, pausing and resuming DHCP service; performing a manual backup of a DHCP server database; migrating the DHCP service from one server to another; manually compacting a DHCP database; monitoring and troubleshooting DHCP; and configuring a DHCP Relay Agent.

Scenario

You are working as a systems administrator at Toynet Inc., a toy retailer with 500 employees. You will be using the DHCP Server service to manage allocation of IP addresses and related configurations of the DHCP clients on your network.

Lesson 4   Implementing and Managing DHCP

Project	Exam 70-291 Objective
4.1 Installing and Authorizing a DHCP Server	Manage DHCP.
4.2 Creating and Managing DHCP Scopes	Manage clients and leases. Manage DHCP scope options.
4.3 Integrating DHCP with DNS	Manage DHCP.
4.4 Performing DHCP Database Maintenance	Manage DHCP. Manage DHCP databases.
4.5 Monitoring and Troubleshooting DHCP	Troubleshoot DHCP. Diagnose and resolve issues related to configuration of DHCP server and scope options.
4.6 Setting up DHCP Relay Agents	Manage DHCP Relay Agent.

General Requirements

To complete the projects in this lesson, you will need administrative rights on two Windows Server 2003 computers connected to the network. You may also find it helpful to refer to Lesson 4 in your Prentice Hall Certification Series Exam 70-291 textbook for further information about the topics covered by the projects in this lesson.

project 4.1

Installing and Authorizing a DHCP Server

exam objective

Manage DHCP.

overview

At any point in time, an average of 50 Toynet employees out of a total of 500 will be working from remote locations. You need to configure Toynet's network to enable the employees outside office premises to connect to the company network from any location, receive correct IP addresses, and work as effectively as they would when in the office. It can be assumed that these employees have their notebook computers configured to obtain IP addresses dynamically.

learning objective

After you have completed this project, you will know how to install the DHCP Server service and authorize a DHCP server.

specific requirements

See general requirements.

estimated completion time

45 minutes

project steps

tip

To add the DHCP Server role from the Manage Your Server window, click Start and click Manage Your Server. Then, click Add or remove a role in the Manage Your Server window.

1. Click **Start**, point to **Control Panel**, and then click **Add or Remove Programs**. The **Add or Remove Programs** window opens.
2. Click **Add/Remove Windows Components**. The **Windows Components Wizard** opens to the **Windows Components** screen.
3. In the **Components** scrolling list box, scroll down to locate **Networking Services** (**Figure 4-1**) and then double-click it to open the **Networking Services** dialog box.
4. Select the **Dynamic Host Configuration Protocol (DHCP)** check box (**Figure 4-2**), and then click **OK**.
5. Click **Next** to advance to the **Configuring Components** screen, where Setup will configure the changes you selected (**Figure 4-3**).
6. If your server has been using a dynamically configured IP address, a message box will open and prompt you to change the address to a static IP address (**Figure 4-4**). Click **OK** to open the **Local Area Connection Properties** dialog box and configure the static IP address (**Figure 4-5**). When you have finished assigning this address and close the Local Area Connection Properties dialog box, the Wizard will complete the Configuring Components phase.
7. Click **Finish** on the **Completing the Windows Components Wizard** screen to close the Wizard.
8. Close the Add or Remove Programs window.
9. Click **Start**, point to **Administrative Tools**, and click **DHCP** to open the **DHCP** console.
10. Right-click **DHCP** in the tree in the left pane of the console window, and then click **Manage Authorized Servers** to open the **Manage Authorized Servers** dialog box.
11. Click **Authorize** to open the **Authorize DHCP Server** dialog box.
12. Type the name or IP address of the DHCP server you wish to authorize in the **Name or IP address** text box (**Figure 4-6**) and click **OK**.
13. The **Confirm Authorization** dialog box opens, displaying the name and IP address of the server you have selected. Click **OK**.
14. Click **Close** to close the Manage Authorized Servers dialog box.
15. Close the DHCP console.

Figure 4-1 Networking Services in the Components scrolling list box

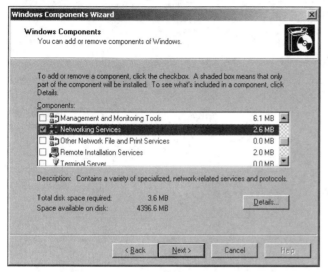

Figure 4-2 Selecting Dynamic Host Configuration Protocol (DHCP)

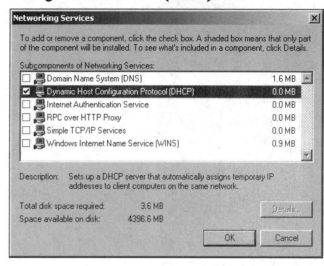

Figure 4-3 Configuring Components screen

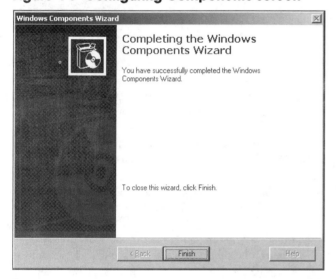

Figure 4-4 Static IP Message Box

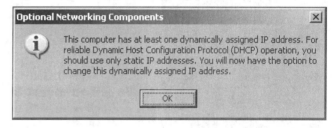

Figure 4-5 Configuring a static IP address

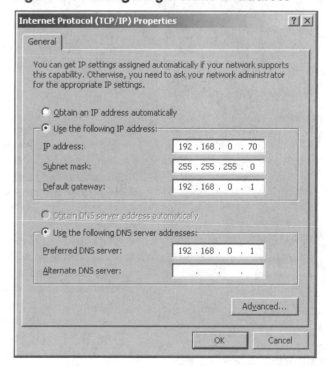

Figure 4-6 The Authorize DHCP Server dialog box

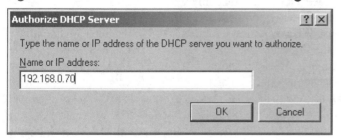

<table>
<tr><td>

project 4.2

</td><td>

Creating and Managing DHCP Scopes

</td></tr>
</table>

exam objective

Manage clients and IP address leases. Manage DHCP scope options.

overview

You must configure a scope that will accommodate Toynet's 500 users of whom an average of 50 are concurrently connected at any one time. You must also exclude the router, and the DHCP server from your range.

learning objective

After completing this project, you will know how to create and manage DHCP scopes on a Windows Server 2003 computer.

specific requirements

To complete this project, you must have completed Project 4.1 (i.e., you must have a Windows Server 2003 computer with the DHCP Server service installed).

estimated completion time

1 hour

project steps

Create and configure a DHCP scope.

1. Open the **DHCP** console.
2. Click the name of your DHCP server in the tree on the left side of the console window.
3. Click **Action** on the Menu bar, and then click **New Scope** to open the **New Scope Wizard**.
4. Click **Next** to open the **Scope Name** screen. Type a name in the **Name** text box that will help you identify the scope easily. Type a description of the scope in the **Description** text box (**Figure 4-7**).
5. Click **Next** to open the **IP Address Range** screen. Type the first address in your DHCP scope in the **Start IP address** text box. Type the last address in the range in the **End IP address** text box.
6. The subnet mask should be set automatically in the bottom half of the IP Address Range screen (**Figure 4-8**). If you need to change the subnet mask, you can specify it in terms of length (number of bits, for example, 24) or as an IP address (for example, 255.255.255.0).
7. Click **Next** to open the **Add Exclusions** screen. On this screen, you can exclude addresses in the specified range from the scope. Exclusions allow you to maintain static addresses within the scope, such as the address of the DHCP server and other servers.
8. In the **Start IP address** text box, type the first address in the address range that you want to exclude from the scope. In the **End IP address** text box, type the last address in the range that you want to exclude from the scope. If you want to exclude only one address, type that address in the Start IP address text box only.
9. Click **Add** to add the range to the **Excluded address range** list box.
10. Click **Next** to open the **Lease Duration** screen (**Figure 4-9**). The default lease duration is 8 days. You can reduce the duration for networks that consist mainly of portable computers and dial-up connections, and increase it for networks that use desktop computers with stable connections. Since Toynet has 500 different computers, with 50 connecting at a time, and it has less than 250 addresses to set aside in this scope, you will want to set a very short lease duration, for example 3 hours or less.
11. Click **Next** to accept the default duration and open the **Configure DHCP Options** screen. If necessary, select the **Yes, I want to configure these options now** option button to configure the IP addresses for default gateways, DNS servers, and WINS servers (**Figure 4-10**).

tip

You can press the period key (.) to begin a new octet in the Start IP address and End IP address text boxes.

caution

Do not proceed with the process of creating scopes if you already have another server running DHCP on the same network segment. You can check for the presence of other DHCP servers by running ipconfig /all or by running the Dhcploc.exe program from the Windows Support Tools folder.

Figure 4-7 Scope Name screen

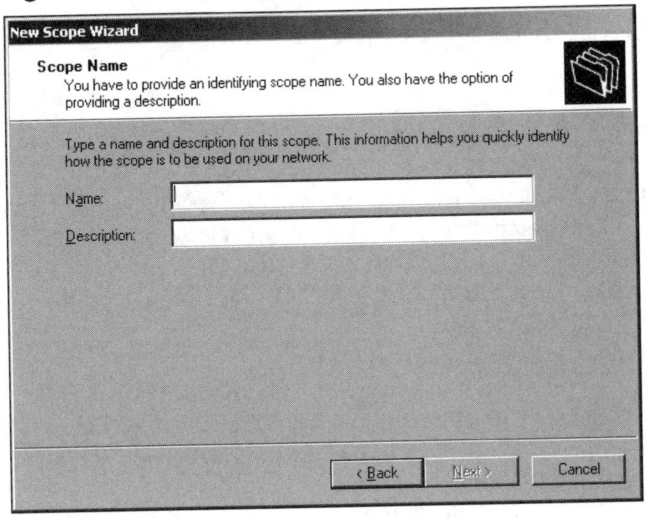

New Scope Wizard

Scope Name
You have to provide an identifying scope name. You also have the option of
providing a description.

Type a name and description for this scope. This information helps you quickly identify
how the scope is to be used on your network.

Name:

Description:

< Back   Next >   Cancel

Figure 4-8 IP Address Range screen

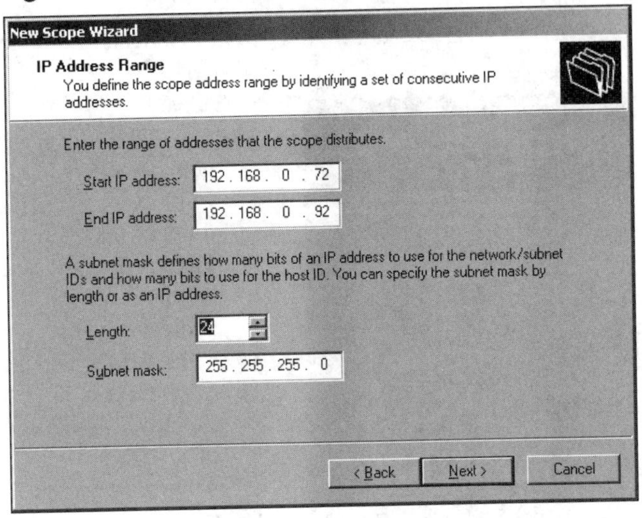

New Scope Wizard

IP Address Range
You define the scope address range by identifying a set of consecutive IP
addresses.

Enter the range of addresses that the scope distributes.

Start IP address: 192 . 168 . 0 . 72

End IP address: 192 . 168 . 0 . 92

A subnet mask defines how many bits of an IP address to use for the network/subnet
IDs and how many bits to use for the host ID. You can specify the subnet mask by
length or as an IP address.

Length: 24

Subnet mask: 255 . 255 . 255 . 0

< Back   Next >   Cancel

Figure 4-9 Lease Duration screen

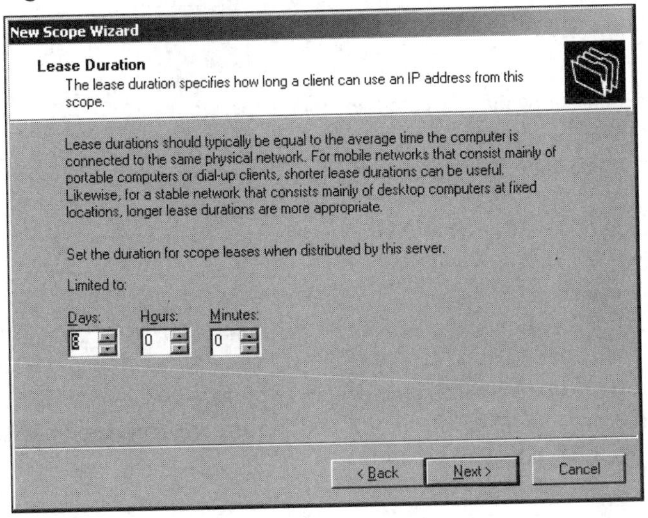

New Scope Wizard

Lease Duration
The lease duration specifies how long a client can use an IP address from this
scope.

Lease durations should typically be equal to the average time the computer is
connected to the same physical network. For mobile networks that consist mainly of
portable computers or dial-up clients, shorter lease durations can be useful.
Likewise, for a stable network that consists mainly of desktop computers at fixed
locations, longer lease durations are more appropriate.

Set the duration for scope leases when distributed by this server.

Limited to:

Days: Hours: Minutes:
8   0   0

< Back   Next >   Cancel

Figure 4-10 Configure DHCP Options screen

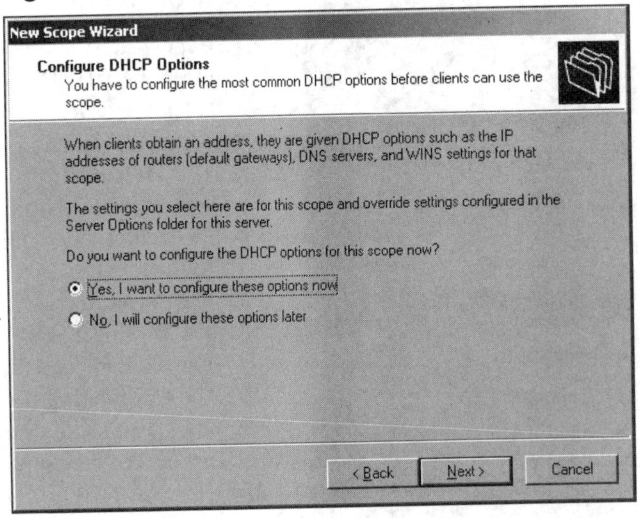

New Scope Wizard

Configure DHCP Options
You have to configure the most common DHCP options before clients can use the
scope.

When clients obtain an address, they are given DHCP options such as the IP
addresses of routers (default gateways), DNS servers, and WINS settings for that
scope.

The settings you select here are for this scope and override settings configured in the
Server Options folder for this server.

Do you want to configure the DHCP options for this scope now?

⦿ Yes, I want to configure these options now

◯ No, I will configure these options later

< Back   Next >   Cancel

project 4.2

Creating and Managing DHCP Scopes (cont'd)

exam objective

Manage clients and IP address leases. Manage DHCP scope option.

project steps

12. Click **Next** to open the **Router (Default Gateway)** screen. Type the address of your network's default gateway in the **IP address** text box and click **Add**.
13. Click **Next** to open the **Domain Name and DNS Servers** screen. Type the name of the domain that you want your client computers to use for DNS name resolution in the **Parent domain** text box. Type the name of the DNS server that you want your scope clients to use in the **Server name** text box and click **Resolve**, or simply type the IP address of the server in the **IP address** text box.
14. Click **Add** to add the server address to the **IP address** list box.
15. Click **Next** to open the **WINS Servers** screen. If you are on a network that is using older Windows clients and NetBIOS name-to-IP address resolution is required, type the name of a WINS server for this scope in the **Server name** text box and click **Resolve**. Alternatively, type the address in the **IP address** text box.
16. Click **Add** to add the WINS server, and then click **Next** to open the **Activate Scope** screen (**Figure 4-11**).
17. Select the **Yes, I want to activate this scope now** option button, if necessary, or click **Cancel** if you are doing this as an exercise only and do not want to create the scope.
18. Click **Next** to open the **Completing the New Scope Wizard** screen.
19. Click **Finish** to complete the creation of the new scope. The new scope is now listed in the DHCP console (**Figure 4-12**).
20. Close the DHCP console.

Many of your remote users now have broadband connections, and as such, they are remaining connected longer. You need more addresses, but are out of room in your current scope. Assuming the network has been supernetted correctly (more than one logical subnet assigned to the same physical subnet), configure another scope and then create a superscope out of the two scopes you created. This way they can be activated and deactivated together.

1. Repeat steps 1 through 20 to create another scope.
2. Open the **DHCP** console.
3. Click the DHCP server on which you want to create the superscope.
4. Click **Action** and then click the **New Superscope** command.
5. The **Welcome to the New Superscope Wizard** screen of the New Superscope Wizard appears. Click **Next**.
6. The **Superscope Name** screen opens (**Figure 4-13**). Type the superscope name in the **Name** text box and click **Next**.
7. The **Select Scopes** screen appears. Click the scope or scopes in the **Available scopes** list box. To select more than one scope, click one scope, press and hold the **[Ctrl]** key and then click the other scopes. Then click **Next**.
8. The **Completing the New Superscope Wizard** screen opens (**Figure 4-14**).
9. Click **Finish** to complete the process of creating and configuring a superscope and display the new superscope in the DHCP MMC snap-in.
10. Close the DHCP Console.

Figure 4-11 Activate Scope screen

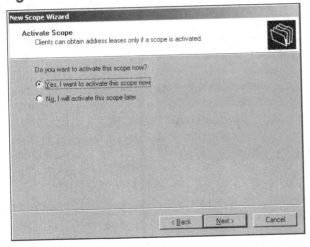

Figure 4-12 DHCP console with new scope

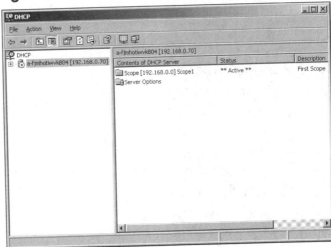

Figure 4-13 Superscope Name screen

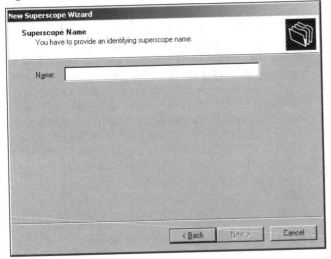

Figure 4-14 Completing the New Superscope Wizard

project 4.3

Integrating DHCP with DNS

exam objective

Manage DHCP.

overview

Client computers need to use the plastic molding injection line monitoring software (an X-Windows-based application hosted on Toynet's Unix server) that Toynet uses to ensure that the latest batch of GI George is being manufactured correctly. In order for this to work, the Unix server must be able to resolve client computers' host names to IP addresses. The Unix server is configured to use your DNS server. In order for the DNS server to resolve the DHCP-enabled clients' host names for the Unix server, you must enable your DHCP server to always update DNS records so that as IP addresses change, the current information is always in DNS. Otherwise, the Unix server can open the X-Windows application on the PC, which can be very confusing to the users.

learning objective

After completing this project, you will know how to integrate DHCP with DNS on a Windows Server 2003 system.

specific requirements

To complete this project, you must have completed projects 4.1 and 4.2.

estimated completion time

10 minutes

project steps

1. Open the **DHCP** console.
2. Right-click the DHCP server that you want to integrate with DNS, and click **Properties** on the shortcut menu to open the **Properties** dialog box for the DHCP server.
3. Click the **DNS** tab and make sure that the **Enable DNS dynamic updates according to the settings below** check box is selected (**Figure 4-15**).
4. You then have the choice of allowing the DHCP clients to determine when their records are updated (i.e., by request), or to update all DHCP client records automatically. Choose the latter option and then click **OK** to close the Properties dialog box.
5. Close the DHCP console.

Figure 4-15 Automatically updating DNS records

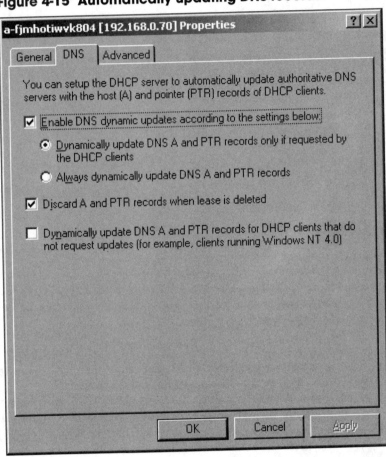

project 4.4 | *Performing DHCP Database Maintenance*

exam objective

Manage DHCP. Manage DHCP databases.

overview

In order to relieve the strain on one of the Toynet domain controllers that currently functions as the DHCP server, you need to move the DHCP Server service to another server. You also want to ensure good performance for the DHCP database, so after moving it you will need to compact it.

learning objective

After you have completed this project, you will know how to pause and resume the DHCP Server service, perform a manual backup of a DHCP server database, migrate the DHCP service from one server to another by moving the DHCP server database, and manually compact the DHCP database.

specific requirements

While this project can be performed with one Windows Server 2003 computer that has DHCP, it is ideal to have two servers.

estimated completion time

30 minutes

project steps

Change the status of a DHCP server, for example, in preparation of a backup.

1. Open the **DHCP** console and select the DHCP server in the console tree.
2. Click **Action** on the Menu bar, point to **All Tasks**, and then click **Pause**.
3. To resume the DHCP service, click **Action**, point to **All Tasks**, and then click **Resume** (**Figure 4-16**).

Perform a manual backup of a DHCP server database.

1. In the console tree of the DHCP console, right-click the server whose database you want to back up and click **Backup** on the shortcut menu.
2. The **Browse for Folder** dialog box opens. The default folder for saving a DHCP database during backup is **%systemroot%\WINDOWS\system32 \dhcp\backup**. You may change this location, but the backup must be saved to a local folder.
3. Click **OK** to save the backup to the specified location. To verify that you have created a backup successfully, navigate to the folder in which you saved the database in Windows Explorer and find the file named **DhcpCfg**, which stores the backup copy of the database. Look at the **Date Modified** data in the details pane of Windows Explorer to verify that the file has just been changed (**Figure 4-17**).

Migrate the DHCP service from one server to another by moving the DHCP server database.

1. Create a manual backup of the current DHCP server database as you did above.
2. Pause the DHCP Server service as described above. Pausing the DHCP server at this point ensures that the server will not grant any new IP address leases to clients or change any other data while you are moving the database.
3. Click **Start**, point to **Administrative Tools**, and then click **Services** to open the **Services** console (**Figure 4-18**).
4. Double-click **DHCP Server** in the details pane to open the **DHCP Server Properties (Local Computer)** dialog box.

Figure 4-16 Resuming the DHCP Server service

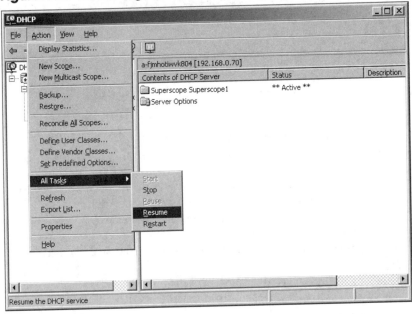

Figure 4-17 The DhcpCfg File

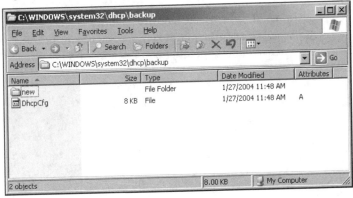

Figure 4-18 The Services console

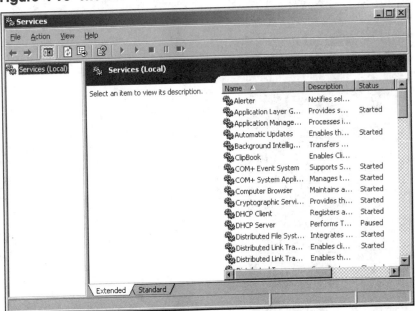

project 4.4

Performing DHCP Database Maintenance (cont'd)

exam objective

Manage DHCP. Manage DHCP databases.

project steps

5. On the **General** tab, click the down arrow in the **Startup type** list box, and then click **Disabled** on the drop-down list (**Figure 4-19**).
6. Click **OK** to close the dialog box and to prevent this DHCP server from starting up again.
7. Copy the folder in which you saved the DHCP server database backup to the computer that will become the DHCP server. (If you only have one server, don't copy it anywhere.)
8. Log on to the computer that will be the new DHCP server as an **Administrator**, make sure that the DHCP Server role is installed, and open the DHCP console.
9. Select the DHCP server in the console tree.
10. Open the **Action** menu, and then click **Restore** (**Figure 4-20**) to open the Browse for Folder dialog box.
11. Select the folder to which you copied the backup of the DHCP database, and then click **OK**. If you are asked if you want to stop and then restart the DHCP service, click **Yes**.

Manually compact the DHCP database.

1. Stop the DHCP Server service.
2. Open a command prompt and navigate to the *%systemroot%*\WINDOWS\system32\dhcp directory by typing **cd \Windows \system32\dhcp** and pressing [**Enter**].
3. Type **jetpack dhcp.mdb compactdhcp.mdb** (**Figure 4-21**) and press [**Enter**]. In this command, **compactdhcp.mdb** is an arbitrary temporary name that you assign to the database.
4. Close the Command Prompt window.
5. Start the DHCP Server service.

Figure 4-19 Disabling a DHCP server

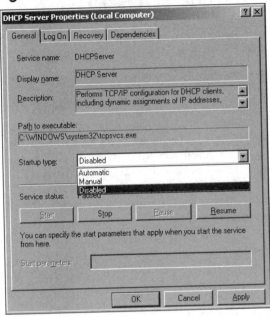

Figure 4-20 Restoring a DHCP database

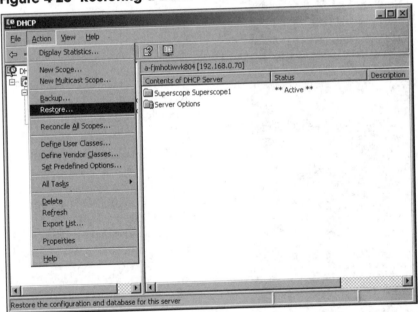

Figure 4-21 Compacting a database with JetPack

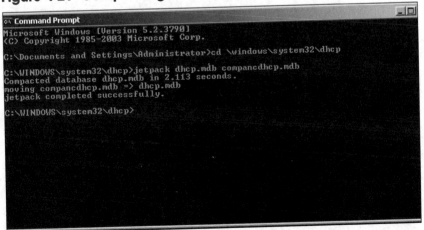

project 4.5

Monitoring and Troubleshooting DHCP

exam objective

Troubleshoot DHCP. Diagnose and resolve issues related to configuration of DHCP server and scope options.

overview

Monitoring the performance of a DHCP server helps both in troubleshooting problems proactively and diagnosing problems after they have occurred. You can monitor the performance of the DHCP Server service by accessing the Server Statistics dialog box (**Figure 4-22**), examining the daily log file that the DHCP Server service maintains of its activities (**Figure 4-23**), and also by examining the DHCP Server's System log (**Figure 4-24**). If you discover a DHCP Server error in the System log, you can double-click it in the details pane to open the Event Properties dialog box for further information (**Figure 4-25**).

learning objective

After completing this project, you will be more familiar with troubleshooting DHCP issues.

specific requirements

To complete this project, you must have completed Projects 4.1 and 4.2.

estimated completion time

10 minutes

project steps

You are receiving a number of complaints that users are not able to access other computers on the network due to non-availability of valid IP addresses. Prepare a report listing a possible solution for each of the following possible causes of the problem.

◆ The DHCP server is multi-homed and not providing service on one or more of its network connections.
◆ Scopes and superscopes not activated or configured on the DHCP server.
◆ The DHCP server located on a different subnet is not providing services to the clients on a remote subnet.
◆ The scope does not have an IP address to lease.
◆ There is a conflict in the IP addresses being offered by two DHCP servers in the network.

Figure 4-22 The Server Statistics dialog box

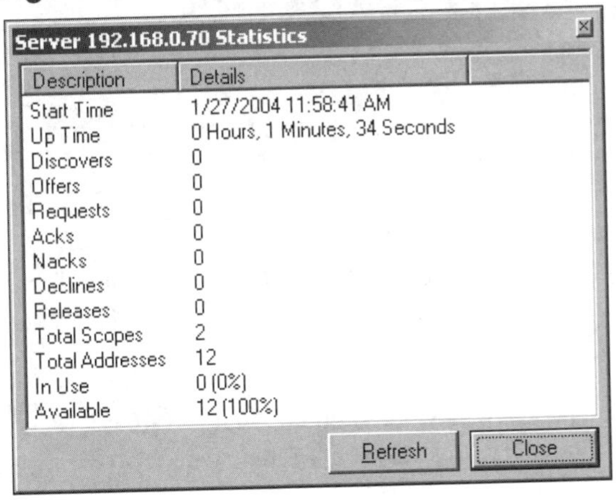

Figure 4-23 DHCP audit log file

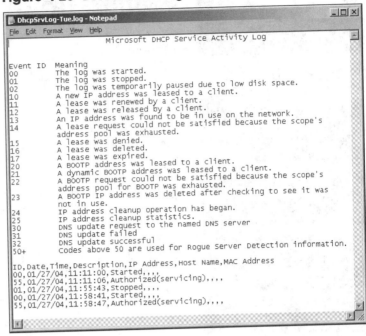

Figure 4-24 System log

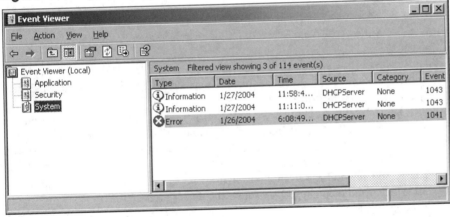

Figure 4-25 The Event Properties dialog box

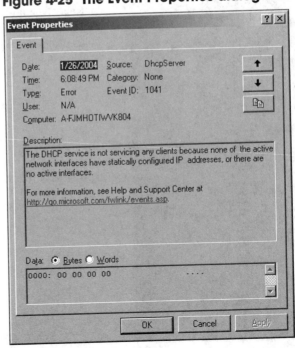

project 4.6

Setting up DHCP Relay Agents

exam objective

Manage DHCP Relay Agent.

overview

Toynet has asked you to set up a new physical subnet and you need to ensure that client computers can get IP addresses from the existing DHCP servers (none of which reside on this subnet).

learning objective

After you have completed this project, you will know how to configure a DHCP Relay Agent on a Windows Server 2003 computer to provide DHCP addresses to remote subnets.

specific requirements

Two Windows Server 2003 computers, one configured as a DHCP server, and the other NOT configured as a DHCP server.

estimated completion time

15 minutes

project steps

1. Log on to a Windows Server 2003 computer that is not your DHCP server as an **Administrator**.
2. Open the **Routing and Remote Access** console.
3. Double-click the name of the server to expand it in the console tree, if necessary, and then similarly expand the **IP Routing** node.
4. Right-click **DHCP Relay Agent** under the **IP Routing** node, and click **Properties** on the shortcut menu to open the **DHCP Relay Agent Properties** dialog box (**Figure 4-26**).
5. Type the IP address of the DHCP server to which you want the relay agent to forward messages in the **Server address** text box.
6. Click **Add** to add the address to the **Server address** list box (you can add additional servers if desired), and then click **OK** to close the dialog box.
7. In the Routing and Remote Access console, right-click **DHCP Relay Agent** again, and this time click **New Interface** on the shortcut menu. The **New Interface for DHCP Relay Agent** dialog box opens.
8. Select the interface through which you want the relay agent to be enabled, in this example the **Local Area Connection (Figure 4-27)**, and click **OK**.
9. Close the Routing and Remote Access console.

Figure 4-26 DHCP Relay Agent Properties dialog box

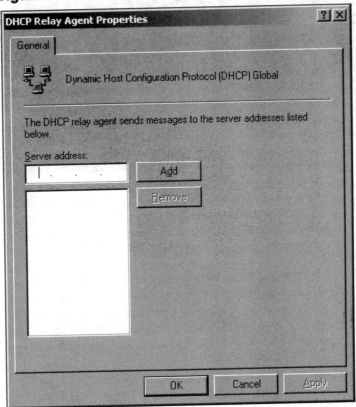

Figure 4-24 New Interface for DHCP Relay Agent dialog box

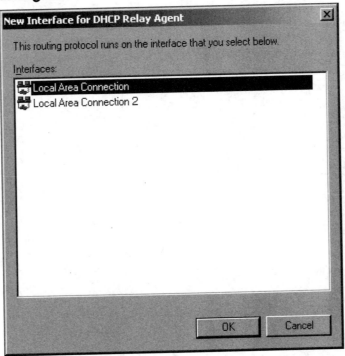

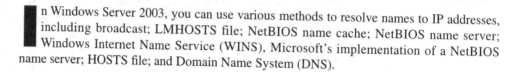

LESSON 5

Understanding Name Resolution and DNS

I n Windows Server 2003, you can use various methods to resolve names to IP addresses, including broadcast; LMHOSTS file; NetBIOS name cache; NetBIOS name server; Windows Internet Name Service (WINS), Microsoft's implementation of a NetBIOS name server; HOSTS file; and Domain Name System (DNS).

Of all the methods used for resolving host names, DNS is the most popular. Aside from its technical features, the main reason for its popularity is that DNS is the naming standard for the Internet. DNS is also an integral part of the Windows Server 2003 operating system. In addition to using DNS to resolve names, Windows uses it to locate different services on the network. Active Directory and many other system functions of Windows Server 2003 depend heavily on the DNS model.

Once you have designed your DNS infrastructure, you can start implementing DNS servers on your network. You designate a Windows Server 2003 computer as a DNS server by installing the Microsoft DNS Server service, also known as adding the DNS Server role.

This lesson includes projects that will let you practice installing the DNS Server service and configuring different client name resolution settings.

Scenario

You are a network administrator for SUV Motors Inc., a regional automobile parts retailer. SUV Motors has 300 users distributed across branch offices in Michigan and Wisconsin and in a main office in Detroit. SUV also has a warehouse in Detroit for spare parts. The company is using a Windows NT-based TCP/IP network for its headquarters and warehouse units. The headquarters is connected to the branch offices using ISDN connections.

Lesson 5   Understanding Name Resolution and DNS

Project	Exam 70-291 Objective
5.1 Installing the DNS Service	Install DNS.
5.2 Confirming Client Name Resolution Settings	Basic knowledge

General Requirements

To complete the projects in this lesson, you will need administrative rights on a Windows Server 2003 computer connected to the network. You may also need the Windows Server 2003 installation CD-ROM. You may also find it helpful to refer to Lesson 5 in your Prentice Hall Certification Series Exam 70-291 textbook for further information about the topics covered by the projects in this lesson.

project 5.1

Installing the DNS Service

exam objective

Install DNS.

overview

SUV Motors has decided to implement Windows Server 2003. The company plans to have a root domain which will have two subdomains, DetroitHQ for its headquarters, and DetroitWA for its warehouse unit. The company wants users to have Internet access as well as quick access to all resources on the network. You have already started with the process of implementing a Windows Server 2003 network and have set up a Windows Server 2003 computer at the headquarters. Now, you have to implement a DNS server on this Windows Server 2003 computer.

learning objective

After completing this project, you will know how to install a DNS server.

specific requirements

See general requirements.

estimated completion time

15 minutes

project steps

1. Log on as an **Administrator**.
2. Click **Start**, point to **Control Panel**, and click **Add or Remove Programs** to open the **Add or Remove Programs** window.
3. Click the **Add/Remove Windows Components** button in order to open the **Windows Components Wizard**. A **Please wait** message appears on the screen while the **Windows Components Wizard** is loaded.
4. Scroll down the **Components** list **(Figure 5-1)** and double-click **Networking Services** to open the **Networking Services** dialog box.
5. Select **Domain Name System (DNS)** on the **Subcomponents of Networking Services** list **(Figure 5-2)**.
6. Click **OK** to close the **Networking Services** dialog box.
7. Click **Next** to open the **Configuring Components** screen. Setup configures the components. This might take a few minutes. If you are prompted, insert your Windows Server 2003 installation CD-ROM, and click **OK**.
8. After the components are configured, the **Completing the Windows Components Wizard** screen opens. Click **Finish**.
9. Close the Add or Remove Programs window.

tip

Before DNS is installed, you need to provide an IP address and DNS address you have not already provided that information previously.

Figure 5-1 The Windows Components screen

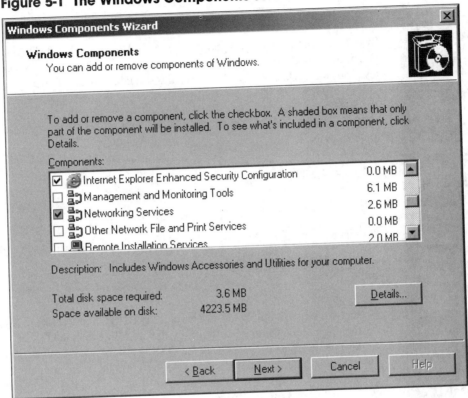

Figure 5-2 Networking Services dialog box

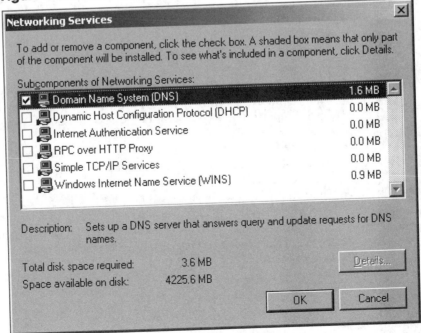

project 5.2

Confirming Client Name Resolution Settings

exam objective

Basic knowledge

overview

SUV Motors has installed a Windows Server 2003 computer as its DNS and WINS server, and you need to confirm that the server itself is set up to resolve names correctly. Corporate IT policy states that HOSTS and LMHOSTS files should not be used unless absolutely necessary.

learning objective

After you have completed this project, you will know how to configure client name resolution settings and be more familiar with how the different name resolution settings can work together.

specific requirements

See general requirements

estimated completion time

15 minutes

project steps

1. Applications and services running on Windows Server 2003 (other than the DNS Server service) will ask the Windows Server 2003 DNS Client service to resolve host names for them. Examine **Figure 5-3** to review the order in which the DNS Client service resolves host names. This is not the way the DNS Server service resolves host names, but it is the same way that the other Windows Server 2003 DNS client computers will resolve host names.

2. Log on as an **Administrator**.

3. Click **Start**, point to **Run** and type **cmd**, then click **OK**. This will open a Command Prompt window.

4. Display this computer's host name by typing **hostname** in the Command Prompt window and pressing **[Enter]**. This is the first thing the DNS Client service examines when asked to resolve a hostname: is it me?

5. Display the contents of the HOSTS file by typing **more %systemroot%\system32 \drivers\etc\hosts** and then pressing **[Enter]**. This is the second place that the DNS Client service will look to resolve names (**Figure 5-4**). Leave the Command Prompt window open.

6. Click **Start**, point to **Control Panel**, point to **Network Connections**, and click **Local Area Connection**. This will open the **Local Area Connection Status** dialog box.

7. Click **Properties** on the **General tab** to open the **Local Area Connection Properties** dialog box.

8. Select the **Internet Protocol (TCP/IP)** option in the **This connection uses the following items** list box and then click the **Properties** button. This will display the **Internet Protocol (TCP/IP) Properties** dialog box (**Figure 5-5**).

9. Enter the server's own IP address as the preferred DNS server. This is the third place the DNS Client service will look to resolve a host name. If it cannot contact the first server in the list then it will try to contact the second server. It does not contact the second server if the first server is contacted but cannot resolve the host name.

10. Delete any other DNS server listings.

tip

When configuring WINS client settings on a WINS server, only the server itself should be listed as its own client's WINS server. No other WINS servers should be listed. This prevents duplicate name registrations in WINS, since the WINS client starts up before the WINS service.

Figure 5-3 Windows Server 2003 methods of resolving host names

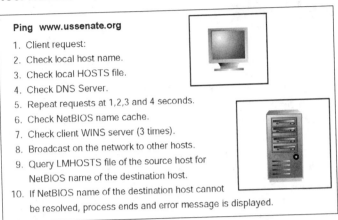

Ping www.ussenate.org

1. Client request:
2. Check local host name.
3. Check local HOSTS file.
4. Check DNS Server.
5. Repeat requests at 1,2,3 and 4 seconds.
6. Check NetBIOS name cache.
7. Check client WINS server (3 times).
8. Broadcast on the network to other hosts.
9. Query LMHOSTS file of the source host for NetBIOS name of the destination host.
10. If NetBIOS name of the destination host cannot be resolved, process ends and error message is displayed.

Figure 5-4 Hostname and HOSTS file

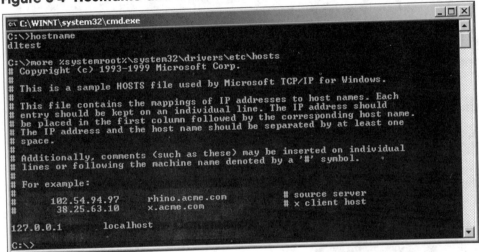

Figure 5-5 Internet Protocol (TCP/IP) Properties dialog box

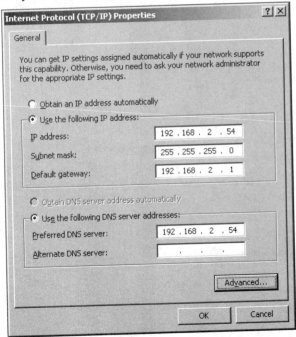

Confirming Client Name Resolution Settings *(cont'd)*

Basic knowledge

11. Display the NetBIOS name cache by switching back to the Command Prompt window and typing **nbtstat –c** and pressing **[Enter]**. This is the fourth place the DNS Client service will look to resolve a host name. (It tries to resolve them by matching up the NetBIOS name to the first part of the host name, before the period.) In **Figure 5-6** you will notice that there is nothing in the NetBIOS name cache. In **Figure 5-7** you will notice three entries for the same server.

12. Click the **Advanced** button and then click the **WINS** tab (**Figure 5-8**).

13. Delete any listings for WINS servers by selecting them and then clicking **Remove**.

14. Click **Add** and type the address of your own server. This is the fifth place that the DNS Client service will look when trying to resolve a host name. Then click **Add** again.

15. Disable LMHOSTS lookup by clearing the **Enable LMHOSTS lookup** check box (**Figure 5-8**).

16. Display the contents of the LMHOSTS file by typing **more %systemroot%\system32 \drivers\etc\Lmhosts** and pressing **[Enter]** in the Command Prompt window. When LMHOSTS Lookup is enabled, this is the last place that the DNS Client service will look. Note that the items that are listed with a #PRE are permanently loaded into the NetBIOS name cache. The other entries are not loaded into cache until they are resolved and then they have a limited lifetime. Compare **Figures 5-6** and **5-7**. In **Figure 5-6** the file does not exist; in **Figure 5-7** the file exists and lists two rows.

Figure 5-6 NetBIOS Name Cache and LMHOSTS File – Empty

Figure 5-7 NetBIOS Name Cache and LMHOSTS File – Not Empty

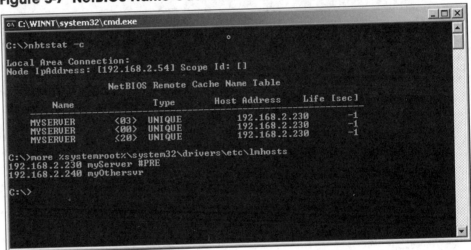

Figure 5-8 The WINS tab

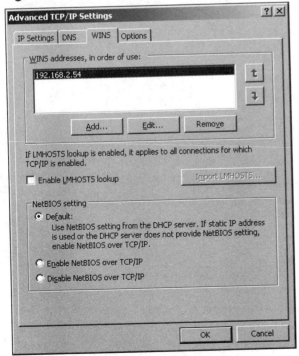

Configuring and Managing a DNS Server

Before you can begin using the DNS server you have installed on your network to map host names to IP addresses, you need to configure the DNS Server. Configuring the DNS Server service mainly involves creating and configuring zones. After you create zones, you can configure them by setting various properties in the DNS console. To make managing your DNS infrastructure easier, you can delegate the administration for parts of a zone to different authorities. You can also configure dynamic updates for zones so that you do not have to update information about resource records manually. In addition to configuring the DNS server, you need to configure DNS clients to refer to a specific DNS server. Otherwise, the DNS clients will not be able to use the services of DNS to resolve host names to IP addresses and vice versa.

Once you have configured the DNS server, you will need to monitor the services that it provides for functionality and performance. You can perform tests to check the DNS Server service by using options provided in the DNS console. Results from these tests will show whether your DNS server is able to handle name resolution requests successfully. After you are sure that your DNS server is functioning, you should start to monitor its performance. Various tools, such as the Performance console and the DNS console, exist for this purpose.

Analysis of data provided by these tools gives you valuable information about the performance of your DNS server. You can use this information to diagnose and eliminate bottlenecks and other issues that are affecting the performance of the server.

This lesson includes projects that will enable you to practice selecting zone types, creating lookup databases, creating a delegated sub-domain, enabling dynamic updates for a DNS zone, testing a DNS server, and monitoring DNS server performance.

Scenario

You are a network administrator for Zeta Car Parts, an automobile car parts manufacturer. Zeta has 200 users distributed across its headquarters and manufacturing unit in Detroit, and 2 branch offices. The company is using a single Windows Server 2003-based TCP/IP network for its headquarters and the manufacturing unit, which is connected to the headquarters using a radio link. A few users at the branch offices use ISDN connections to connect to the headquarters. The domain structure of Zeta Motors has a root domain, which has one sub-domain, for its brakes unit. All users on the network have access to the Internet. You have already installed a DNS server on the Windows Server 2003 computer at the headquarters. The next step in this process is to configure the DNS Server.

Lesson 6   Configuring and Managing a DNS Server

Project	Exam 70-291 Objective
6.1 Configuring the DNS Server Service	Install and configure DNS Server Service.
6.2 Creating Delegated DNS Zones	Configure DNS zone options.
6.3 Configuring DNS Zones for Dynamic Updates	Configure DNS zone options.
6.4 Testing a DNS Server	Monitor DNS.
6.5 Monitoring DNS Server Performance	Monitor DNS.

General Requirements

To complete the projects in this lesson, you will need administrative rights on a Windows Server 2003 computer with the DNS Server service installed and connected to a network. You may also find it helpful to refer to Lesson 6 in your Prentice Hall Certification Series Exam 70-291 textbook for further information about the topics covered by the projects in this lesson.

| project 6.1 | *Configuring the DNS Server Service* |

| exam objective | Install and configure DNS Server Service. |

| overview | You will use the Configure Your Server Wizard to install and configure DNS on your server with a forward lookup zone and a reverse lookup zone. |

| learning objective | After completing this project, you will know how to select zone types and create lookup databases. |

| specific requirements | See general requirements. |

| estimated completion time | 45 minutes |

| project steps | |

1. Log on as an **Administrator**, click **Start**, point to **Administrative Tools**, and then click **DNS** to open the **DNS** console.
2. Click the name of the DNS server in the console tree.
3. Click **Action** on the **Menu** bar, and then click **Configure a DNS Server**.
4. The **Welcome to the Configure a DNS Server Wizard** screen appears (**Figure 6-1**). Click **Next**.
5. The **Select Configuration Action** screen appears (**Figure 6-2**). Select the **Create forward and reverse lookup zones (recommended for large networks)** option button, and click **Next**.
6. The **Forward Lookup Zone** screen appears (**Figure 6-3**).
7. Leave the **Yes, create a forward lookup zone now (recommended)** option button selected, and click **Next**.
8. The **Zone Wizard** appears. Leave the **Primary Zone** option selected and click **Next**.
9. The **Zone Name** screen appears (**Figure 6-4**). Type **ZetaCarParts.com** in the **Zone Name** text box, and click **Next**.
10. The **Zone File** screen appears. Leave the **Create a new file with this file name: (ZetaCarParts.com.dns)** option button selected, and click **Next**.
11. The **Dynamic Update** screen appears. Leave the selected default option, **Do not allow dynamic updates**, and click **Next**.
12. The **Reverse Lookup Zone** screen appears (**Figure 6-5**). Leave the default option, **Yes, create a reverse lookup zone now**, selected, and click **Next**.
13. The **Zone Type** screen appears. Leave the **Primary Zone** option selected and click **Next**.
14. The **Reverse Lookup Zone Name** screen appears. Type your network ID, for example 192.168.2, in the **Network ID** text box (**Figure 6-6**). Then click **Next**.
15. The **Zone File** screen appears. Approve the default name for your zone file by clicking **Next**.
16. The **Dynamic Update** screen appears. This time, select **Allow both non-secure and secure dynamic updates**, and click **Next**.
17. The **Forwarders** screen appears. Leave the **No, it should not forward queries** option button selected, and click **Next**.
18. The **Completing the Configure a DNS Server Wizard** screen appears. After reviewing the settings, click **Finish**.
19. The **Configure Your Server Wizard** reappears. Click **Finish**.
20. Close the **Manage Your Server** window.

Figure 6-1 Welcome to the Configure a DNS Server Wizard

Figure 6-2 Select Configuration Action screen

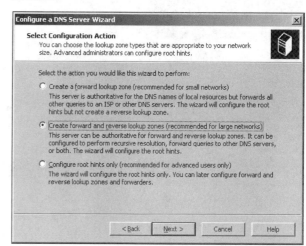

Figure 6-3 Forward Lookup Zone screen

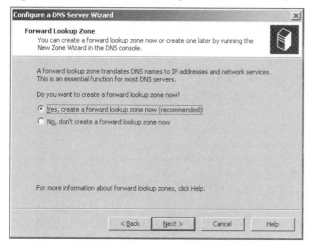

Figure 6-4 Zone Name screen

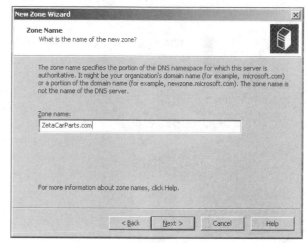

Figure 6-5 Reverse Lookup Zone screen

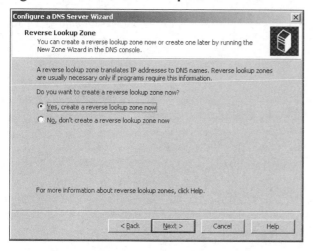

Figure 6-6 Reverse Lookup Zone Name screen

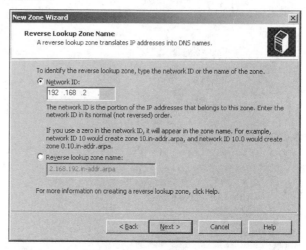

project 6.2 · *Creating Delegated DNS Zones*

exam objective

Configure DNS zone options.

overview

The Brakes division of Zeta Car Parts has determined a business need to have a distinct identity from the other divisions while remaining under the Zeta Car Parts umbrella. You must create a delegated sub-domain of ZetaCarParts.com called Brakes.ZetaCarParts.com.

learning objective

After completing this project, you will know how to create a delegated sub-domain.

specific requirements

To complete this project, you must have completed Project 6.1.

estimated completion time

15 minutes

project steps

1. Open the **DNS** console.
2. Right-click the zone **ZetaCarParts.com**, and then click **New Delegation** on the shortcut menu. The **New Delegation Wizard** opens.
3. Click **Next** to open the **Delegated Domain Name** screen **(Figure 6-7)**. You use this screen to create a sub-domain, the authority for which will be delegated to a different zone.
4. In the **Delegated domain** text box, type the name of the sub-domain, **Brakes**, which will be created under ZetaCarParts.com and will delegate its authority to another name server. Note that the FDQN appears below in a grayed out text box.
5. Click **Next** to open the **Name Servers** screen **(Figure 6-8)**. This screen enables you to specify the DNS name server that will host the delegated zone.
6. Click **Add** to open the **New Resource Record** dialog box **(Figure 6-9)**. In the **Server name** text box, type the name of the DNS server that will host the delegated zone, **ns1.zetacarparts.com**. In the **IP address** text box, enter the IP address of the DNS server (in a production situation, this would be an existing DNS server).
7. Click **OK** to close the **New Resource Record** dialog box and add the chosen DNS name server to the Name servers list on the Name Servers screen.
8. Click **Next** to open the **Completing the New Delegation Wizard** screen, where you can view a summary of the settings you have selected.
9. Click **Finish** to close the wizard. You will now be able to see the sub-domain that you created under the selected zone. The sub-domain contains a Name Server (NS) record for the name server that will host the delegated zone.
10. Close the DNS console.

Figure 6-7 Delegated Domain Name screen

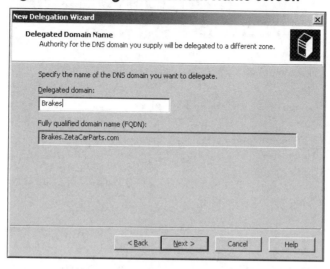

Figure 6-8 Name Servers screen

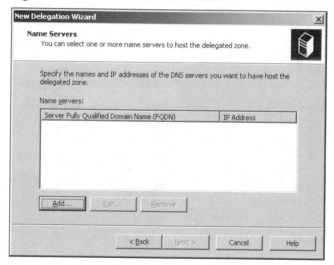

Figure 6-9 New Resource Record dialog box

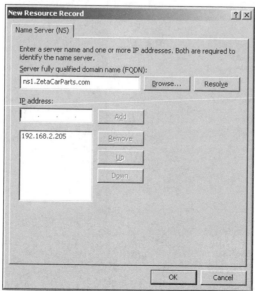

project 6.3

Configuring DNS Zones for Dynamic Updates

exam objective

Configure DNS zone options.

overview

Now that Zeta Car Parts has upgraded all of their client computers to operating systems that support dynamic updates, you want to do away with the manual process of updating the DNS zones, by enabling dynamic updates for the ZetaCarParts.com zone and its sub-domain Brakes.

learning objective

After completing this project, you will know how to enable dynamic updates for a DNS zone.

specific requirements

To complete this project, you must have completed Projects 6.1 and 6.2.

estimated completion time

10 minutes

project steps

1. Open the **DNS** console.
2. Right-click the **ZetaCarParts.com** zone, and then click **Properties** on the shortcut menu to open the **Properties** dialog box for the zone.
3. Click the **General** tab, if it is not already in view.
4. Click the **Dynamic updates** drop-down list box, and then click the **Nonsecure and secure** option to select it **(Figure 6-10)**.
5. Click **OK** to close the **Properties** dialog box.
6. Repeat steps 2 through 5, clicking the Brakes zone to enable dynamic updates for the Brakes sub-domain.
7. Close the DNS console.

Figure 6-10 Zone Properties—Dynamic Updates

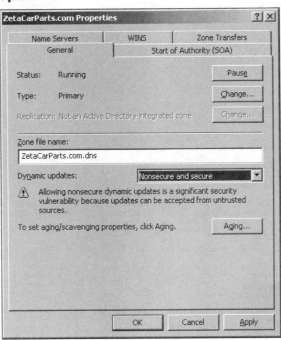

project 6.4

Testing a DNS Server

exam objective

Monitor DNS.

overview

After implementing DNS, you need to test it to ensure that the DNS server is working properly. You will use the options available in the DNS console to test the DNS server by sending a simple query.

learning objective

After completing this project, you will know how to perform a simple test to validate the basic setup of your DNS Server service.

specific requirements

See general requirements.

estimated completion time

5 minutes

project steps

1. Open the **DNS** console.
2. Right-click the DNS server that you want to test, and then click the **Properties** command to open the **Properties** dialog box.
3. Click the **Monitoring** tab. You will use the options in this tab to test your DNS server by sending a query to the DNS server (**Figure 6-11**).
4. Select the **A simple query against this DNS server** check box to test the DNS server.
5. Click the **Test Now** button to send the simple query to your DNS server. The result of the query appears in the **Test Results** box.
6. Click **OK** to close the Properties dialog box and return to the DNS console.
7. Close the DNS console.

Figure 6-11 Monitoring tab—Simple Query

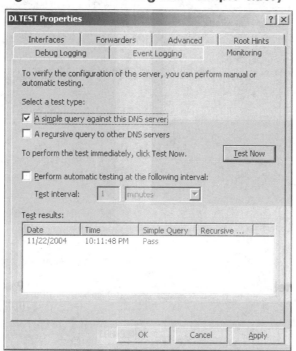

project 6.5

Monitoring DNS Server Performance

exam objective

Monitor DNS.

overview

After you have implemented DNS, the users on your network are complaining about the delays in resolution of DNS queries. To identify the cause of the problem, you need to analyze the performance of your DNS server for 15 minutes. In order to do this, you plan to track relevant performance counters by using the System Monitor.

learning objective

After completing this project, you will know how to monitor DNS server performance.

specific requirements

See general requirements.

estimated completion time

30 minutes

project steps

1. Click **Start**, point to **Administrative Tools**, and then click the **Performance** command. The **Performance** console window appears.
2. Select **System Monitor** to track the DNS performance counters.
3. Click **Add** on the System Monitor toolbar to open the **Add Counters** dialog box.
4. Select the **DNS** option from the **Performance object** list box (**Figure 6-12**). The performance counters related to DNS appear in the **Select counters from list** scroll box.
5. Add all of the DNS counters by selecting the **All Counters** option button.
6. Click **Close** to close the **Add Counters** dialog box. This displays the graph based on the data collected by the selected set of performance counters in the Performance console window (**Figure 6-13**).
7. Observe this data for 15 minutes, while performing simple tests (see Project 6.4), or using Nslookup to perform tests. Eliminate some of the counters that appear to have no activity. Focus on those that display activity.
8. Close the Performance console window.

Figure 6-12 Add Counters dialog box

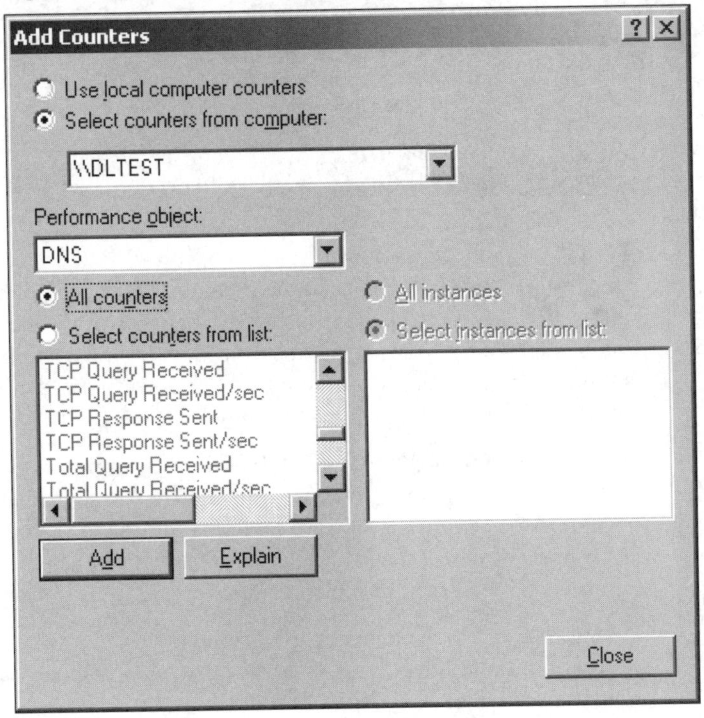

Figure 6-13 Performance Monitor Window

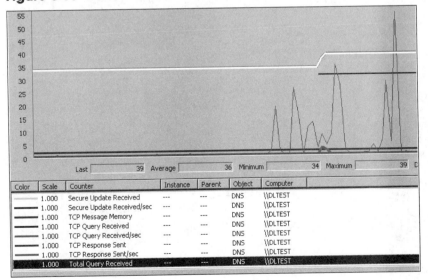

Implementing and Managing WINS

Windows Internet Name Service (WINS) is a naming service that resolves NetBIOS names to the IP addresses of computers on a TCP/IP-based network. If you happen to work with a network from which older operating systems have been phased out, you may not require the WINS service at all. However, many networks still contain computers running versions of Windows such as Windows 98, Windows NT, and Windows ME that make WINS necessary.

To begin the implementation of WINS, you need to install the WINS service on a Windows Server 2003 computer, which will enable the computer to function as a WINS server. In addition to configuring a WINS server on the network, you will need to enable the clients on the network to use the WINS server for NetBIOS name resolutions. Once configured to access the WINS server, the client computers will function as WINS clients.

Windows Server 2003 enables you to configure a DNS server to query the WINS databases for name resolution if the DNS server is unable to resolve a host name-to-IP address query using its own database.

This lesson contains projects that will let you practice installing a WINS server and configuring a DNS zone for WINS lookups.

Scenario

You are working as the network administrator of SuperSoft Inc., a company that deals in providing solutions for a variety of software applications. You recently installed several Windows Server 2003 computers on your network. One of these computers is configured as a DNS server. The network also contains 50 computers running Windows Me, which use NetBIOS names for communication. Additionally, the network hosts 100 computers running Windows 2000 Professional, Windows NT 4.0 Workstation, and Unix. The Unix computers host X-Windows applications that run on the Windows NT 4.0 Workstations. As the network administrator, you need to make sure that there is smooth communication between the computers on your network.

Lesson 7   Implementing and Managing WINS

Project	Exam 70-291 Objective
7.1 Installing a WINS Server	Basic knowledge
7.2 Configuring a WINS Client	Basic knowledge
7.3 Configuring the DNS Service to Perform WINS Lookups	Configure DNS zone options.

General Requirements

To complete the projects in this lesson, you will need administrative rights on a Windows Server 2003 computer connected to a network that is also a DNS server. You also will need administrative rights on a Windows 2000 or Windows XP Professional Client computer. Additionally, you must have completed the projects in Lesson 6 (or have a DNS server with a forward lookup zone and a reverse lookup zone configured). You may also find it helpful to refer to Lesson 7 in your Prentice Hall Certification Series Exam 70-291 textbook for further information about the topics covered by the projects in this lesson.

project 7.1

Installing a WINS Server

exam objective

Basic knowledge

overview

To begin the implementation of WINS, you need to install the service on a Windows Server 2003 computer, which will enable the computer to function as a WINS server. A WINS server is a NetBIOS name server (NBNS), which is server software dedicated to resolving NetBIOS names to IP addresses. An NBNS contains a database file that can accept dynamic NetBIOS name-to-IP address registrations and answer queries for NetBIOS name resolutions. As an NBNS, a WINS server hosts a WINS database for registration and resolution of client NetBIOS name-to-IP address queries.

learning objective

After completing this project, you will know how to install a WINS server.

specific requirements

See general requirements.

estimated completion time

10 minutes

project steps

1. Click **Start**, point to **Administrative Tools**, and then click the **Manage Your Server**. This will display the **Manage Your Server** screen (**Figure 7-1**).
2. Click **Add or remove a role**.
3. The **Preliminary Steps** screen appears. Click **Next** to move on to the **Server Role** screen (**Figure 7-2**).
4. Click **WINS server** and click **Next**.
5. The **Summary of Selections** screen appears. Click **Next** to install the WINS service. After installation is complete, the **This Server is Now a WINS Server** screen appears (**Figure 7-3**). Before clicking **Finish**, follow the instructions below.
6. Click the blue link titled **View the next steps for this role** to display Windows 2003 Help information about WINS.
7. When you're done perusing Help, close it.
8. Click the blue link titled **Configure Your Server log** in order to display in **Notepad** a text-based log of actions taken using the Configure Your Server Wizard (**Figure 7-4**). When you're done examining, close Notepad.
9. Click **Finish** to return to the Manage Your Server screen.
10. Close the **Manage Your Server** screen.

tip

The importance of WINS is greatly diminished in Windows Server 2003 networks. However, it may still be needed to support pre-Windows 2000 clients and other non-Windows NetBIOS clients.

Figure 7-1 Manage Your Server screen

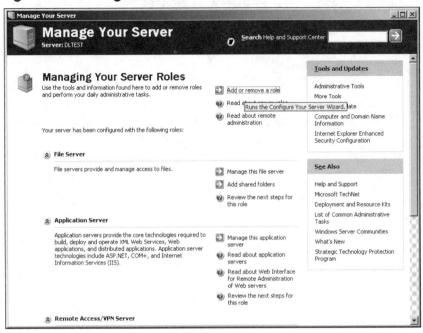

Figure 7-2 Server Role screen

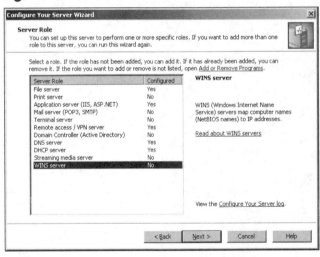

Figure 7-3 This Server is Now a WINS Server screen

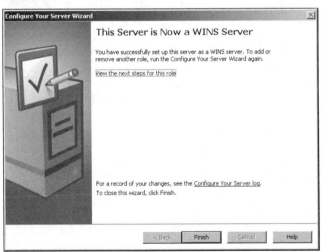

Figure 7-4 Configure Your Server log

project 7.2   *Configuring a WINS Client*

exam objective

Basic knowledge

overview

After installing a WINS server, you need to configure WINS clients to use the WINS server for NetBIOS name resolution. To configure a WINS client, you assign the client the IP address of the WINS server to which the client can send its name resolution queries. This direct querying of a WINS server is preferable to using broadcasts to resolve NetBIOS names because it reduces network traffic.

learning objective

After completing this project, you will know how to configure a WINS client.

specific requirements

See general requirements.

estimated completion time

10 minutes

project steps

1. Log on to a Windows 2000 or Windows XP Professional client computer as an **Administrator**.
2. Open the **Local Area Connection Properties** dialog box.
3. On the **General** tab, select **Internet Protocol (TCP/IP)** in the **This connection uses the following items** list box. Then click **Properties** to open the **Internet Protocol (TCP/IP) Properties** dialog box.
4. On the **General** tab of the Internet Protocol (TCP/IP) Properties dialog box, click **Advanced** to open the **Advanced TCP/IP Settings** dialog box. Then click the **WINS** tab (**Figure 7-5**).
5. On the WINS tab, click **Add** to open the **TCP/IP WINS Server** dialog box (**Figure 7-6**).
6. Type the IP address of the desired WINS server in the **WINS server** text box, and then click **Add**. The WINS server you have selected is added to the **WINS addresses, in order of use** list box on the WINS tab. This is the WINS server that the client will query for NetBIOS name resolution.
8. Close all open dialog boxes and windows.

Figure 7-5 The WINS tab in the Advanced TCP/IP Settings dialog box

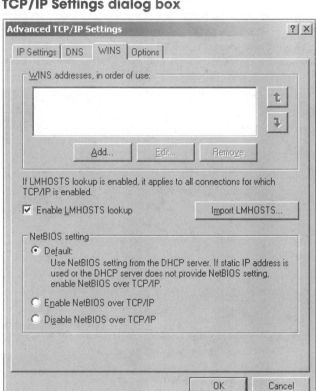

Figure 7-6 The TCP/IP WINS Server dialog box

project 7.3

Configuring the DNS Service to Perform WINS Lookups

exam objective

Configure DNS zone options.

overview

SuperSoft is using a non-Windows Server 2003 computer to provide DHCP addresses to the network (which includes Windows NT 4.0 workstations). The Unix computers host X-Windows applications, which must be able to resolve the host names on the Windows NT 4.0 workstations to IP addresses. Since Windows NT 4.0 workstations cannot update DNS dynamically, and neither can the Unix computer provides IP addresses through DHCP, or query WINS, you must configure WINS lookup in your DNS zone.

learning objective

After completing this project, you will know how to configure a zone for WINS lookup.

specific requirements

To complete this project, you must have completed Project 7.1 and have an existing zone in your DNS server.

estimated completion time

15 minutes

project steps

1. Open the **DNS** console.
2. Right-click the zone **ZetaCarParts.com** (or whatever your zone name is), and then click **Properties** on the shortcut menu. This will display the **Properties** dialog box for the zone.
3. Click the **WINS** tab (**Figure 7-7**).
4. Check the **Use WINS forward lookup** check box.
5. Type the IP address of your WINS Server and click **Add**, then click **OK**.
6. Then navigate to the reverse lookup zone you created earlier.
7. Right-click the reverse lookup zone and then click **Properties** on the shortcut menu. This will display the **Properties** dialog box for the reverse lookup zone.
8. Click the **WINS-R** tab (**Figure 7-8**).
9. Check the **Use WINS-R lookup** check box.
10. In the **Domain to be appended to return name** text box, type **ZetaCarParts.com**.
11. Click **OK**. This configures the reverse lookup zone to query the WINS server configured on the WINS tab of the forward lookup zone ZetaCarParts.com, and then to append the domain name ZetaCarParts.com to the host name as the FQDN.

Figure 7-7 WINS tab

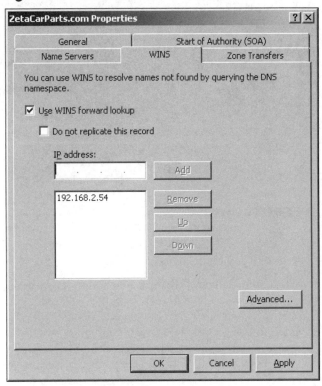

Figure 7-8 WINS-R tab

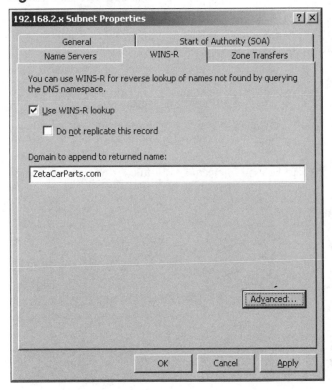

Implementing Remote Access

To access resources on your organization's LAN from a remote location, you can use Windows Server 2003's Routing and Remote Access Service (RRAS). You can configure an RRAS server to perform the functions of a network router, to provide Remote Access Services (RAS), as a VPN server, or to provide shared Internet access.

When you configure RRAS to function as a dial-in remote access server, telecommuters, employees whose jobs involve traveling, and other remote employees can connect to their office networks and access resources. A remote access server is a Windows Server 2003 computer with RRAS enabled that is configured specifically to function using a modem, or a modem pool, to allow users to dial-in from laptops or any other remote computers that are also configured with a modem. Users can then access their e-mail, scheduling, and file and printer sharing services. A VPN server is another type of remote access server.

These methods utilize authentication protocols that are negotiated during the connection process. To be authenticated, the user provides a set of credentials that may be sent in either plain text or encrypted depending upon the authentication protocol used.

After a remote user has completed the authentication process, a well-designed remote access solution must determine if the actual connection is allowed. This is known as authorizing the connection. Windows Server 2003 uses information in the user account's dial-in properties as well as remote access policy settings to determine if the connection will be allowed or denied.

In addition to authenticating and authorizing remote users, protecting the data that is sent between the user and the company's private network is also critical. Data protection can be accomplished by encrypting data using virtual private network protocols. Point-to-Point Tunneling Protocol (PPTP) with Microsoft's Point-to-Point Encryption (MPPE) protocol or Layer 2 Tunneling Protocol (L2TP), which incorporates Internet Protocol Security (IPSec), can be used to create secure tunnels over a public network such as the Internet. Data sent through these tunnels is encrypted.

Scenario

You are the network administrator of TellWire Inc. Your company has provided users with remote access to the network through the Internet. Now, you plan to improve the security of your network while remote users access it. To do this, you need to provide authentication to users who are accessing the network as well as ensure data encryption.

Lesson 8 Implementing Remote Access

Project	Exam 70-291 Objective
8.1 Configuring Routing and Remote Access Security	Manage remote access. Configure remote access authentication protocols.
8.2 Using Encryption Protocols for Data Security	Manage remote access. Implement secure access between private networks.
8.3 Managing Devices and Ports	Manage remote access. Manage devices and ports.

General Requirements

To complete these projects, you will need administrative rights on a Windows Server 2003 computer with RRAS enabled and configured for LAN and demand-dial routing (see Project 3.4), and at least one remote access policy already configured. You may also find it helpful to refer to Lesson 8 in your Prentice Hall Certification Series Exam 70-291 textbook for further information on the topics covered by the projects in this lesson.

project 8.1

Configuring Routing and Remote Access Security

exam objective

Manage remote access. Configure remote access authentication protocols.

overview

You have given your users remote access to the company network, using an Internet connection. However, you realize that this increases security risks. Allowing unfettered remote access enables anyone to access the connection to your network and misuse resources on it. Therefore, you decide that only authenticated users, such as sales representatives, will have access to the network. To do so, you need to enable an authentication protocol to authenticate remote access. Since the remote sales representatives supply their own laptops and software, you will be supporting a wide variety of remote access clients, including some non-Microsoft clients. Therefore, you must support CHAP (non-Microsoft clients), MS-CHAP, and MS-CHAP v2.

learning objective

After completing this project, you will know how to enable the CHAP, MS-CHAP, and MS-CHAP v2 authentication protocols to authenticate remote users to access your network resources.

specific requirements

See general requirements.

estimated completion time

15 minutes

project steps

1. Log on to the computer as an **Administrator**.
2. Click **Start**, point to **Administrative Tools**, and then click **Routing and Remote Access** to open the **Routing and Remote Access** console.
3. Click the server name for which you want to enable authentication protocols.
4. Right-click the server icon and select **Properties**.
5. In the *<Server_name>* **Properties** dialog box, click the **Security tab (Figure 8-1)** to provide authentication to remote access clients and demand-dial routers.
6. Click the **Authentication Methods** button to open the **Authentication Methods** dialog box.
7. Select the **Encrypted authentication (CHAP)**, the **Microsoft encrypted authentication version 2 (MS-CHAP v2)**, and the **Microsoft encrypted authentication (MS-CHAP)** check boxes to enable encryption of clients' user names and passwords.
8. Click **OK** to enable the CHAP authentication protocols and close the Authentication Methods dialog box **(Figure 8-2)**.
9. Click **OK** to close the *<Server_name>* **Properties** dialog box.
10. Click **Close** to close the Routing and Remote Access console.

tip

Enabling authentication protocols at the server level enables RAS policies to use these methods, but it does not force them to accept these methods.

**Figure 8-1 Security tab in RRAS Server
Properties dialog box**

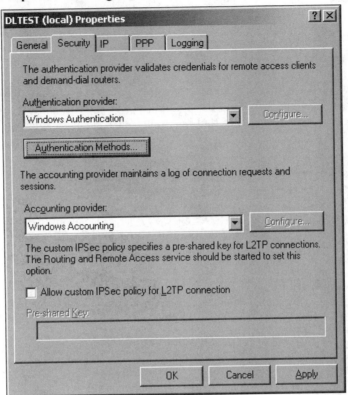

Figure 8-2 Authentication Methods dialog box

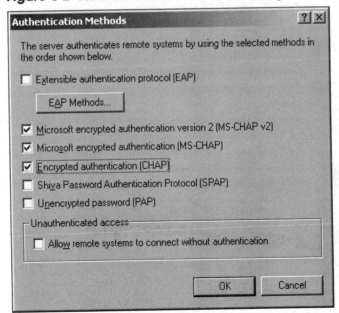

project 8.2

Using Encryption Protocols for Data Security

exam objective

Manage remote access. Implement secure access between private networks.

overview

You have given remote access to users using a dial-up connection and have enabled the authentication protocols to authenticate users accessing TellWire's network. However, you are concerned about the possibility that hackers might intercept the data while it is being transferred. Therefore, you want the data to be encrypted using the strongest possible encryption protocols. However, since the remote sales representatives supply their own laptops and software, you are still supporting a wide variety of remote access clients. Therefore, you must support Basic Encryption, Strong Encryption, and Strongest Encryption. You also need to develop a report for management showing how this leaves your network exposed.

learning objective

After completing this project, you will know how to configure encryption protocols in the profile settings for a remote access policy.

specific requirements

See general requirements. In addition, you will need at least one remote access policy already configured. If you do not, refer to Project 9.2.

estimated completion time

10 minutes

project steps

1. Open the **Routing and Remote Access** console.
2. Double-click the server name to expand it on the console tree.
3. Click **Remote Access Policies** to view the list of remote access policies in the right pane.
4. In the right pane, right-click the policy for which you want to configure the encryption protocols, and select **Properties (Figure 8-3)**. This displays the properties of that RAS policy (**Figure 8-4**).
5. Click the **Edit Profile** button to open the **Edit Dial-in Profile** dialog box.
6. Click the **Encryption** tab (**Figure 8-5**) to apply encryption settings for the selected policy.
7. Make sure that all options are selected except for the **No Encryption** check box to ensure that encryption of the data must be used by RAS clients.
8. Click **OK** to set the encryption settings and close the Edit Dial-in Profile dialog box.
9. Click **OK** to close the Properties dialog box.
10. Click **Close** to close the Routing and Remote Access window.
11. Create a table in Excel and list the encryption methods supported.
12. In another column, list the number of bits used.
13. In another column, list the number of combinations this creates (2 to the power of the number of bits), i.e. 10-bit would be 1024 combinations.
14. In the next column, list the time to crack for 40-bit (use 1 hr). For the others, divide the possible combinations by the possible combinations for 40-bit and then multiply by the time to crack 40-bit encryption.
15. In order to make the data more digestible, add a column called Years. In this column, convert the hours to years by dividing by (24*365).
16. Then, copy the table for a "what if scenario." Assuming computers got 1000 times faster, change the time to crack 40-bit to be 1 hr divided by 1000.
17. Repeat Step 16 at one million and one trillion times faster.

Figure 8-3 RRAS console—Remote access policy context menu

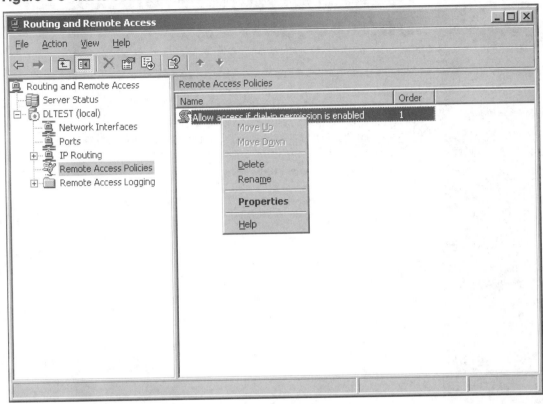

Figure 8-4 RAS Policy Properties dialog box

Figure 8-5 Encryption tab in the Edit Dial-in Profile dialog box

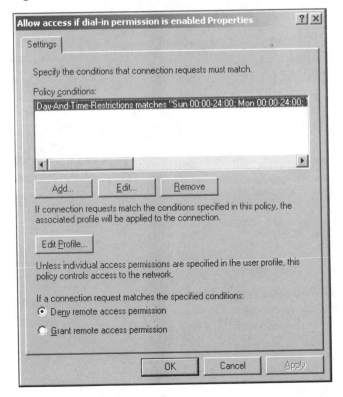

project 8.2

Using Encryption Protocols for Data Security (cont'd)

Manage remote access. Implement secure access between private networks.

project steps

18. You will see that 128-bit encryption remains impervious to brute force attacks even if computers were one trillion times faster (35 billion years). Whereas, 40-bit encryption is currently vulnerable, and 56-bit encryption could easily be vulnerable with some technology advances (**Table 8-1**).

Table 8-1   Time to Crack Encryption

Type	Bits	Possible Combinations	Time to crack on very fast computers using brute force (hrs)	Years
Basic	40	1.09951E+12	1	0.000114155
Strong	56	7.20576E+16	65536	7.481278539
Strongest	128	3.40282E+38	3.09485E+26	3.53293E+22
What if computers get 1,000 times faster?				
Basic	40	1.09951E+12	0.001	1.14155E-07
Strong	56	7.20576E+16	65.536	0.007481279
Strongest	128	3.40282E+38	3.09485E+23	3.53293E+19
What if computers get 1,000,000 times faster?				
Basic	40	1.09951E+12	0.000001	1.14155E-10
Strong	56	7.20576E+16	0.065536	7.48128E-06
Strongest	128	3.40282E+38	3.09485E+20	3.53293E+16
What if computers get one trillion (1,000,000,000,000) times faster?				
Basic	40	1.09951E+12	1E-12	1.14155E-16
Strong	56	7.20576E+16	6.5536E-08	7.48128E-12
Strongest	128	3.40282E+38	3.09485E+14	35,329,339,021

project 8.3 | *Managing Devices and Ports*

exam objective

Manage remote access. Manage devices and ports.

overview

You just discovered that someone has been dialing into the analog 56k modem that you have installed in the Windows Server 2003 computer. Until you get a chance to set up a secure RAS policy, you must disable inbound connections on this modem.

learning objective

After completing this project, you will know how to enable and disable RRAS ports.

specific requirements

See general requirements and the tip below.

estimated completion time

10 minutes

project steps

1. Open the **Routing and Remote Access** console.
2. Double-click the server name to expand it in the console tree.
3. Right-click **Ports** and then click **Properties** to open the **Ports Properties** dialog box (**Figure 8-6**).
4. Select the modem and then click **Configure** to open **the Configure Device** dialog box (**Figure 8-7**).
5. Clear the **Remote Access Connections (inbound only)** check box.
6. Click **OK** to close the Configure Device dialog box.
7. Click **OK** to close the Ports Properties dialog box.
8. Close the RRAS console.

tip

If your computer does not have a modem, use the PPTP ports instead. Or you can add a standard 56 Kbps modem through the Control Panel (even if you don't have a physical modem).

Figure 8-6 Ports Properties dialog box

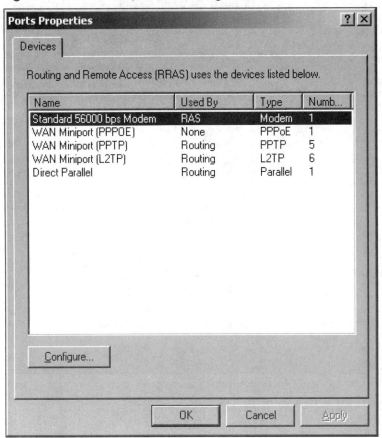

Figure 8-7 Configure Device dialog box

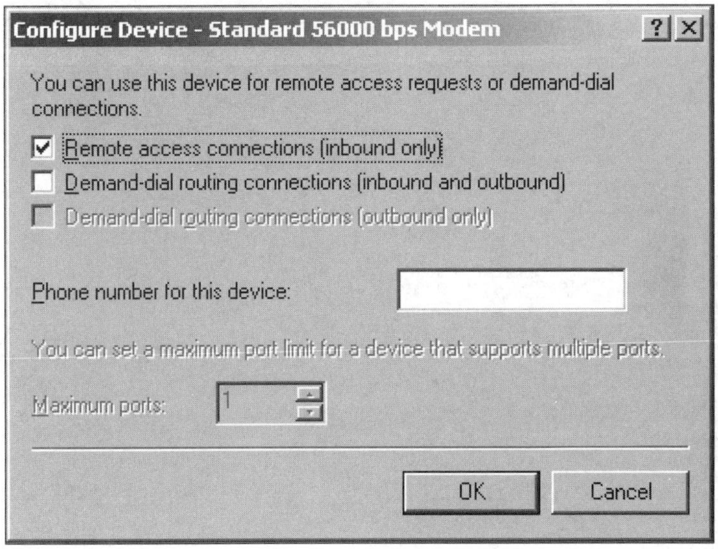

Managing Remote Access

Remote access policies are perhaps the most complicated component of RRAS for the administrator new to Windows 2000 and Windows Server 2003. Remote access policies are highly flexible and powerful, but this power and flexibility also makes them a bit complex.

This lesson includes projects that will help you become familiar with how the various components of remote access policies are applied, and enable you to practice configuring remote access conditions and profile settings, configuring a RADIUS server and RADIUS clients, and auditing remote access security events.

Scenario

You are the brand new network administrator of Tell Nobody Accounting Inc. (soon to be bigger than the Big Four accounting firms). You will need to understand the remote access policies in place, implement some new ones, see to the company's need for growth, and monitor it for problems.

Lesson 9   Managing Remote Access

Project	Exam 70-291 Objective
9.1 Applying Remote Access Policies	Manage Routing and Remote Access clients.
9.2 Configuring Conditions and Profile Settings	Manage Routing and Remote Access clients.
9.3 Configuring Internet Authentication Service (IAS)	Configure Internet Authentication Service (IAS) to provide authentication for Routing and Remote Access clients.
9.4 Monitoring Remote Access Security	Troubleshoot user access to remote access services.

General Requirements

To complete the projects in this lesson, you will need administrative rights on a Windows Server 2003 computer with RRAS enabled. You may also find it helpful to refer to Lesson 9 in your Prentice Hall Certification Series Exam 70-291 textbook for further information on the topics covered by the projects in this lesson.

project 9.1

Applying Remote Access Policies

exam objective

Manage Routing and Remote Access clients.

overview

Your predecessor left a confusing mess of remote access policies that deliver inconsistent results, but fortunately he left some documentation for you, including a plain-English explanation of what he meant to accomplish.

learning objective

After completing this project, you will know how the various components of remote access policy apply.

o specific requirements

See general requirements.

estimated completion time

15 minutes

project steps

1. Examine the documentation for the four remote access policies (**Table 9-1**).
2. Examine the setups for the 5 typical users (**Table 9-2**).
3. Determine which policy will apply to which user and what will happen. Use **Figure 9-1** to help you.
4. Prepare a report illustrating these findings and what needs to be done to make each policy work the way it is supposed to work.

Table 9-1   Policy Documentation

Name	Description
Policy #1: Healthy Managers	Allow managers to connect after business but limit them to 2 hours
Permissions	Allow access
Conditions	Windows-Groups matches, Value: Managers. Day and Time Restrictions, Value: Sun-Sat 5 PM - 12 AM
Profile	Dial-in Constraints: Allow access only on these days and at these times: Sun-Sat 5 PM - 12 AM
Policy #2: SweatShop Accounting	Allow Accounting to connect whenever, from wherever, and for however long, with maximum security
Permissions	Deny access
Conditions	Windows-Groups matches, Value: Acctg
Profiles	Authentication, MS-CHAP v2. Encryption: Strongest Encryption
Policy #3: HR Remote Access	Allow HR to access the network at any time for up to 2 hrs
Permissions	Deny access
Conditions	Windows-Groups matches, Value: HR
Profile	Session Timeout, Value 120
Policy #4: Domain Users RAS	Allow domain user access if dial-in permission allowed and using a secure, MS-CHAP v2 authentication
Permissions	Deny access
Conditions	Authentication Type, Value: MS-CHAP v2
Profile	Default Settings

Table 9-2   User List

Username	Groups	Dial-In Settings	Typical Connections
DSmith	Acctg, Domain Users, Managers	Control Access Through Remote Policy, Always Callback to (911) 911-9110	Dials up from home number (911) 911-9110 around 9 PM and 7 AM
AJones	Acctg, Domain Users	Control Access Through Remote Policy	Dials up from home number (911) 911-9112 around 9 PM from Windows 95 PC (that has never been patched)
FFarragut	Domain Users, HR	Control Access Through Remote Policy	Connects over cable during business hours
GCooper	Acctg, Domain Users, Managers	Allow Access	Dial up from various hotels between 7 PM and 8 PM and 6 AM and 7 AM
SDooper	Acctg, Domain Users, Managers	Assign a static IP address 10.1.23.234, Deny Access	Connects over cable during business hours

Figure 9-1 RAS Policy Chart

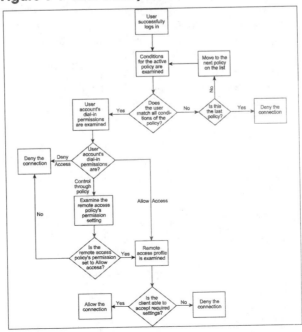

project 9.2

Configuring Conditions and Profile Settings

exam objective

Manage Routing and Remote Access clients.

overview

Tell Nobody's management is concerned that too many employees are losing work life balance and are working too many hours. They want you to restrict remote access to the network to the hours of 6 AM until 8 PM, Monday through Friday, and they want connections to last no longer than 8 hours. Then, realizing that they need you on call 24/7, they ask you to enable your access without restriction.

learning objective

After you have completed this project, you will know how to configure conditions and profile settings.

specific requirements

See general requirements.

estimated completion time

15 minutes

project steps

1. Click **Start**, point to **Administrative Tools**, and then click **Routing and Remote Access** to open the **Routing and Remote Access** console.
2. Double-click the server name to expand it on the console tree.
3. Click **Remote Access Policies** to view the list of remote access policies in the right pane.
4. Right-click the blank space in the right pane and select **New Remote Access Policy** (**Figure 9-2**). This displays the **Welcome** screen of the **New Remote Access Policy Wizard**.
5. Click **Next** to advance to the **Policy Configuration Method** screen (**Figure 9-2**).
6. Select **Set up a custom policy** and then name your policy **WorkAholic Prevention**. Click **Next**.
7. On the **Policy Conditions** screen, click **Add** to open the **Select Attributes** dialog box and select the attributes that will make up the policy (**Figure 9-4**).
8. Double-click **Windows-Groups** to open the **Groups** dialog box.
9. Click **Add** to open the **Select Groups** dialog box. Enter the name of the group for which you want to set the new remote access policy (in this example the group is named Workaholics—you may need to create your own Workaholics group, or select another group of your own choosing). Click **Add**.
10. Click **OK** to close the Select Groups dialog box and then click **OK** again to close the Groups dialog box. Then click **Next**.

tip

When a new RAS connection is attempted, the Remote Access Service hunts through the policy list until it finds the first policy that it matches. It must match all of the attributes specified in the policy.

Figure 9-2 New Remote Access Policy command

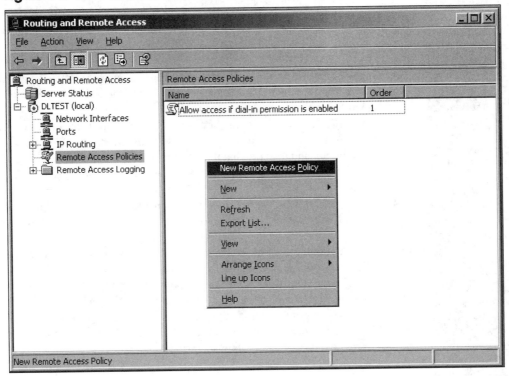

Figure 9-3 Policy Configuration Method screen

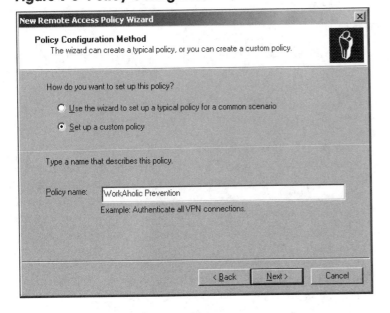

Figure 9-4 Adding attributes to the policy conditions

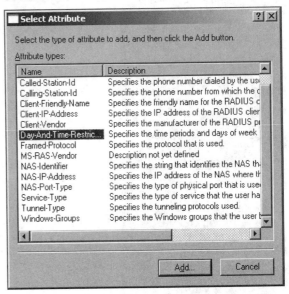

<table>
<tr><td>**project 9.2**</td><td>*Configuring Conditions and Profile Settings (cont'd)*</td></tr>
<tr><td>**exam objective**</td><td>Manage Routing and Remote Access clients.</td></tr>
<tr><td>**project steps**</td><td>

11. On the **Permissions** screen, select **Grant remote access permission** and then click **Next**.
12. On the **Profile** screen, click **Edit Profile**. Check the **Allow Access only on these days and at these times** check box, then click the **Edit** button.
13. The **Dial-in Hours** dialog box appears. Allow users to connect Monday through Friday from 6 AM to 8 PM by moving the mouse to the Monday 6 AM box, pressing down the mouse button and then moving it to the Friday 8 PM box before releasing the mouse button. Then select the **Permitted** option button and the selected area will turn blue (**Figure 9-5**). Click **OK**.
14. In the **Edit Dial-in Profile** dialog box, check the **Minutes client can be connected (Session-Timeout)** check box and enter **480** in the spin box (**Figure 9-6**). Then click **OK**.
15. Click **Next** in the **Profile** screen to advance to the **Completing the New Remote Access Policy Wizard** screen. Then click **Finish**.
16. Set the encryption of the profile of the policy to require encryption (see Project 8.2).
17. To view the properties of the your own user account to make sure you are allowed access, open the **Computer Management** console. Navigate to **Users and Groups**, and then to **Users**. Right-click on your user account and click **Properties**. Then view the setting and if necessary, change it to **Allow access (Figure 9-7)**.

</td></tr>
</table>

Figure 9-5 Dial-in Hours dialog box

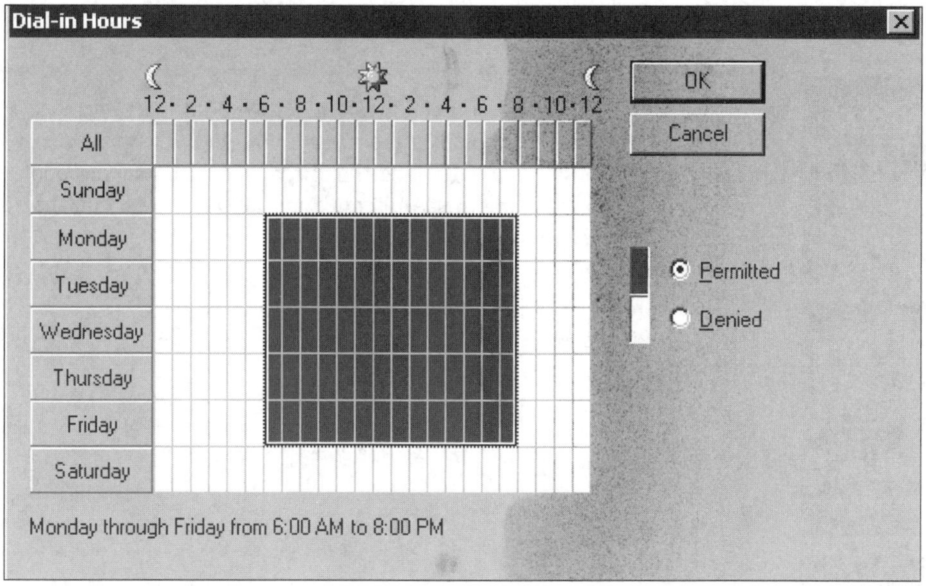

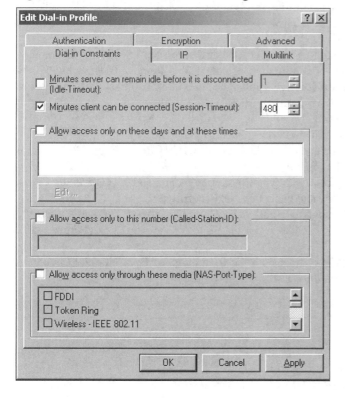

Figure 9-6 Edit Dial-in Profile dialog box

Figure 9-7 Remote Access Permissions settings in the Properties dialog box for a user account

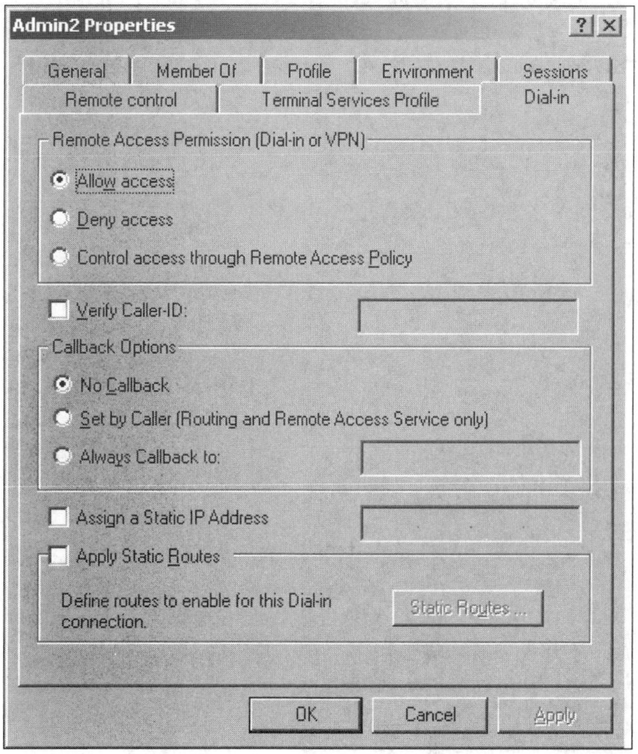

project 9.3

Configuring Internet Authentication Service (IAS)

exam objective

Configure Internet Authentication Service (IAS) to provide authentication for Routing and Remote Access clients.

overview

Apparently, someone told somebody about Tell Nobody's remote access capabilities because your RAS users have doubled in the last month, and you will need to add another remote access server. Before adding an additional remote access server, and a VPN appliance you will need to configure Internet Authentication Service (IAS) on the current remote access server so that users will get consistent results, no matter which remote access server handles their request.

learning objective

After completing this project, you will be able to configure a RADIUS server and RADIUS clients.

specific requirements

See general requirements.

estimated completion time

10 minutes

project steps

1. Log on as an **Administrator**.
2. Click **Start**, click **Control Panel**, and then click **Add or Remove Programs**.
3. Click the **Add/Remove Windows Component** button in the **Add or Remove Programs** window to start the **Windows Components Wizard**.
4. In the **Windows Components Wizard**, double-click **Networking Services** to open the **Networking Services** dialog box.
5. Check the check box to the left of **Internet Authentication Service**, click **OK** and then click **Next**. When prompted, click **Finish**. Close the Add or Remove Programs window.
6. Click **Start**, point to **Administrative Tools**, and then click **Internet Authentication Service** to open the **Internet Authentication Service** console.
7. Right-click **Internet Authentication Service**, and then click **Register Server in Active Directory**. Then click **OK** in the **Server registered** dialog box.
8. Right-click **RADIUS Clients** and then click **New RADIUS Client** **(Figure 9-8)** to open the **New RADIUS Client** dialog box.
9. Enter **Nortel VPN Appliance** in the **Friendly name** text box and **10.1.2.1** in the **Client address (IP or DNS)** text box and then click **Next (Figure 9-9)**.
10. In the **Additional Information** dialog box, select **Nortel Networks** as the **Client-Vendor** and enter a shared secret in the **Shared secret** text box **(Figure 9-10)**. Then click **Finish**.
11. Create an additional RADIUS Client with the friendly name **RAS NG**, the IP address **10.45.6.1**, and **RADIUS Standard** as the Client-Vendor.

Figure 9-8 New RADIUS Client command

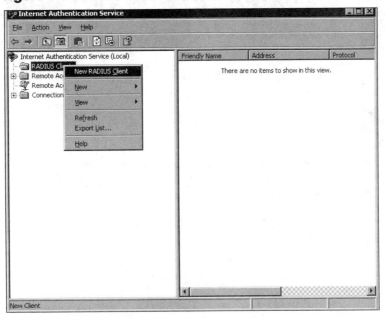

Figure 9-9 New RADIUS Client dialog box

Figure 9-10 Additional Information dialog box

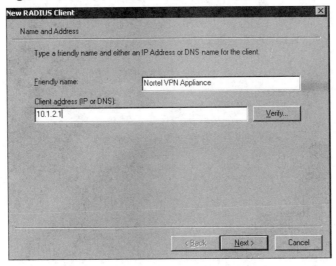

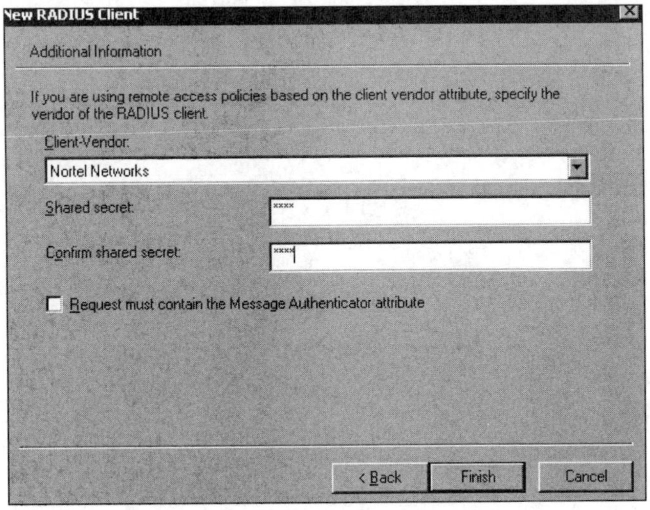

project 9.3

Configuring Internet Authentication Service (IAS) (cont'd)

exam objective

Configure Internet Authentication Service (IAS) to provide authentication for Routing and Remote Access clients.

project steps

Configure a RADIUS client (if you don't have another Windows Server 2003 computer to use, just reuse the first one).

12. Open the **Routing and Remote Access** console.

13. Right-click the name of the server in the left hand pane and click **Properties**.

14. Click the **Security** tab and change the Authentication provider to **RADIUS Authentication (Figure 9-11)**.

15. Click the **Configure** button. This opens the **RADIUS Authentication** dialog box **(Figure 9-12)**.

16. Click the **Add** button. The **Add RADIUS Server** dialog box opens. Enter the DNS name of the server you configured **(Figure 9-13)**.

17. Click the **Change** button. The **Change Secret** dialog box opens. Enter the shared secret you used when you set up RAS NG as a client on the RADIUS server. (See Step 10 on page 9.10.) **(Figure 9-14)**.

18. Click **OK** several times to accept the changes.

19. When prompted to restart RRAS, click **OK**.

Figure 9-11 Selecting RADIUS authentication

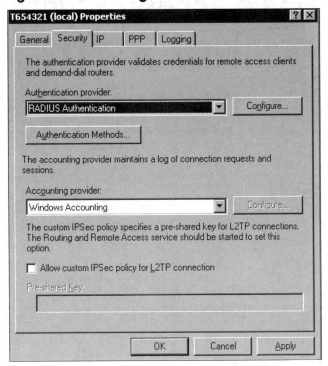

Figure 9-12 RADIUS Authentication dialog box

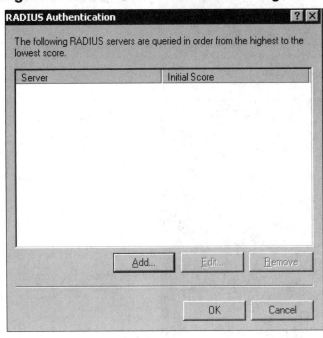

Figure 9-13 Adding a RADIUS Server on the client

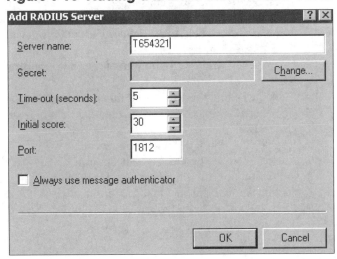

Figure 9-14 Change Secret dialog box

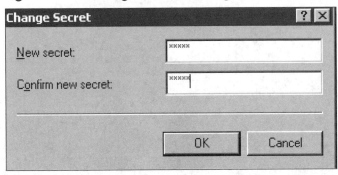

project 9.4 | *Monitoring Remote Access Security*

exam objective

Troubleshoot user access to remote access services.

overview

You have authenticated remote users to access Tell Nobody's network and encrypted the information that is transferred between the client and the server. You now want to audit system events and audit account logon events, to check for security breaches. To do this, you first need to enable the Security Log to log these events in Event Viewer. This will also aid in troubleshooting connections.

learning objective

After you have completed this project, you will know how to audit remote access security events.

specific requirements

See general requirements.

estimated completion time

5 minutes

project steps

1. Click **Start**, point to **Administrative Tools**, and click **Local Security Policy** to open the **Local Security Settings** console.
2. Click the plus sign to the left of **Local Policies** to expand the list of local policies. Then in the left pane, click **Audit Policy**. This will display the available events to audit in the details pane (**Figure 9-15**).
3. Double-click **Audit system events** to open the **Audit system events Properties** dialog box.
4. Click the **Define these policy settings** check box.
5. Check the **Failure** check box to audit the failure of system events (**Figure 9-16**). Then click **OK**.
6. Double-click **Audit account logon events**.
7. Click the **Define these policy settings** check box.
8. In the **Audit account logon events Properties** dialog box, click **Success** and **Failure** to audit both successful and failed logon attempts.
9. Click **OK** to close the Properties dialog box and the close the Local Security Settings console.

Figure 9-15 Enabling Auditing

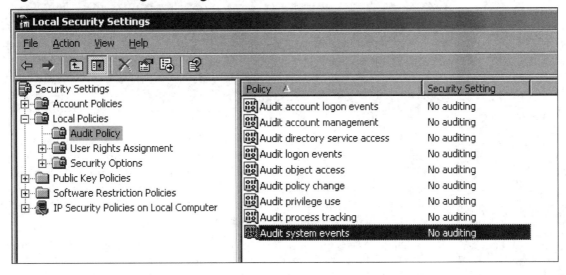

Figure 9-16 Auditing the failure of system events

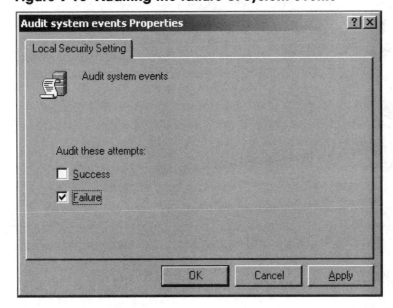

10 Implementing and Managing Certificate Services

A Public Key Infrastructure (PKI) consists of protocols, standards, and technologies that provide both authentication and encryption services. Using Windows Certificate Services, you can implement your own Public Key Infrastructure, which will allow you to strengthen authentication by utilizing smart cards, protect data in transit by using the services of Internet Protocol Security (IPSec), or even protect data stored on local hard drives using Encrypting File System (EFS).

Computers, users, and services use certificates as a way of identifying themselves on the network. Certificates are digital credentials that are issued by a Certification Authority (CA), which vouches for their validity. The information contained in each certificate is dictated by the X.509 standards.

By installing Certificate Services on a Windows Server 2003 computer, you can configure your own CA. In addition to issuing certificates, CAs also manage the certificates to maintain the integrity of the PKI. Some networks will have only one CA, while others will have multiple CAs configured in what is known as a certification hierarchy. There are two types of CAs: Enterprise and Standalone. You manage Certificate Services through the Certification Authority console.

Certificates are obtained by using enrollment Web pages or by using the Certification Request Wizard. Although Enterprise CAs offer both options, a Standalone CA only allows certificate enrollment by using Web pages.

The projects included in this lesson will enable you to practice installing a Standalone root CA, and viewing, renewing and revoking a certificate.

Scenario

You are the CIO of NoHassleNetworksISP Inc. Your company is undergoing a rigorous security certification process, performed by Ridiculously Rigorous Security Certification Inc. (RRSC). They have determined that you need to shift your VPN technology (which connects your branch offices to headquarters) from PPTP to L2TP. This is mandated because L2TP using IPSec provides proof of the data's integrity and it also authenticates the originating computer, not just the originating user. Consequently, you need to set up a Public Key Infrastructure so that you can issue certificates to enable L2TP's use of IPSec.

Lesson 10 Implementing and Managing Certificate Services

Project	Exam 70-291 Objective
10.1 Implementing a Certification Authority (CA)	Basic knowledge
10.2 Working with Certificates	Basic knowledge

General Requirements

To complete the projects in this lesson, you will need administrative rights on a Windows Server 2003 computer with IIS installed and Web publishing enabled. It can be a domain member or a standalone server. You may also find it helpful to refer to Lesson 10 in your Prentice Hall Certification Series Exam 70-291 textbook for further information about the topics covered by the projects in this lesson.

project 10.1

Implementing a Certification Authority (CA)

exam objective

Basic knowledge

overview

Ridiculously Rigorous Security Certification, Inc. has helped you determine that using a Windows Server 2003 computer as your root CA is quite acceptable. The L2TP certificates will be installed on only one Windows Server 2003 computer in each location. Each will serve as a VPN router. Consequently, a Standalone CA, as opposed to an Enterprise CA, is required. This will also allow you greater security by being able to take the root CA offline.

learning objective

After completing this project, you will know how to install a Standalone root CA.

specific requirements

See general requirements.

estimated completion time

30 minutes

project steps

1. Log on as an **Administrator**.
2. Click **Start**, point to **Control Panel**, and click the **Add/Remove Programs** icon to open the **Add/Remove Programs** window.
3. Click the **Add/Remove Windows Components** icon to open the **Windows Components** screen of the **Windows Components Wizard**. This wizard will guide you through the process of installing a Standalone CA.
4. In the **Windows Components** screen (**Figure 10-1**), select the **Certificate Services** check box. As you check the box, a warning message will appear (**Figure 10-2**).
5. The message warns you that, after installation, you cannot change the machine name nor can you change its domain membership, as this would invalidate certificates issued by the machine. Click **Yes** to continue.
6. Click **Next** to start the installation process for Certificate Services. The **CA Type** screen appears (**Figure 10-3**).
7. Click the **Stand-alone root CA** option button to install a Standalone root CA and then click **Next**.
8. The **CA Identifying Information** screen opens (**Figure 10-4**). In the **Common name for this CA** box, type the name of the server. In the **Distinguished name suffix**, use X.509 naming syntax to enter information (i.e. O=NoHassle,OU=ISP). Then click **Next**.
9. The **Generating Cryptographic keys** screen appears briefly, then disappears on its own.
10. The **Certificate Database Settings** screen opens (**Figure 10-5**). Accept the defaults for the database settings and commence the rest of the installation process by clicking **Next**
11. On the **Completing the Windows Components Wizard** screen, click **Finish**.

Figure 10-1 Windows Components screen

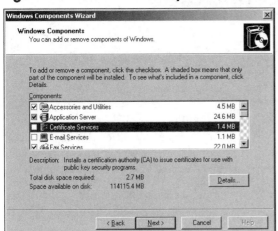

Figure 10-2 Warning message

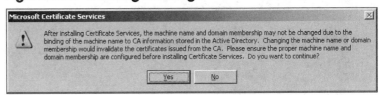

Figure 10-3 CA Type screen

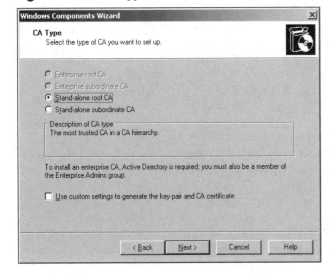

Figure 10-4 CA Identifying Information screen

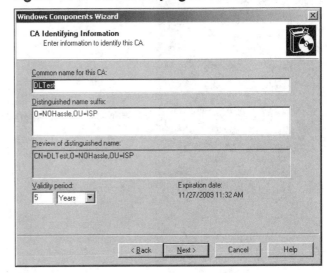

Figure 10-5 Certificate Database Settings screen

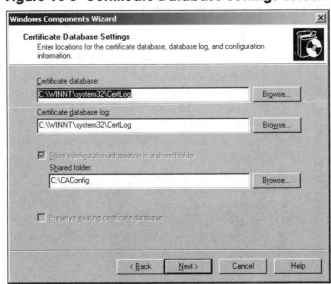

<table>
<tr><td>**project 10.2**</td><td># *Working with Certificates*</td></tr>
<tr><td>**exam objective**</td><td>Basic knowledge</td></tr>
<tr><td>**overview**</td><td>First, you must review the certificate for No Hassle's CA. Then, you must issue a certificate in preparation for installing the VPN routers. A while later, you notice the certificate of the root CA is about to expire, so you must renew it in advance. After a break-in occurs at one of your remote offices, you discover that a VPN router server was stolen and you must revoke its certificate.</td></tr>
<tr><td>**learning objective**</td><td>After completing this project, you will know how to view, issue, renew and revoke a certificate.</td></tr>
<tr><td>**specific requirements**</td><td>To complete this project, you must have completed Project 10.1.</td></tr>
<tr><td>**estimated completion time**</td><td>35 minutes</td></tr>
</table>

project steps

View the certificate of a Standalone root CA.

1. Log on as an **Administrator**.
2. Click **Start**, point to **Administrative Tools**, and then click **Certification Authority**. This opens the **Certification Authority** console.
3. In the left pane, select the server. Right-click the server and then click the **Properties** command to open the *<Certificate_Name>* **Properties** dialog box (**Figure 10-6**).
4. Click the **View Certificate** button in the *<Certificate_Name>* **Properties** dialog box to view the certificate (**Figure 10-7**). The **General** tab displays three main properties of the certificate. These properties are: **Issued to**, **Issued by**, and **Valid from**.
5. To see more properties, click the **Details** tab in the *<Certificate_Name>* **Properties** dialog box to see detailed information about the certificate, such as the Public Key of the certificate, the Signature Algorithm being used by certificate, the Version of the certificate, Serial Number, etc.
6. Click **OK** to close the *<Certificate_Name>* **Properties** dialog box.

tip

You can also open the Properties dialog box for a certificate by selecting the server and then selecting the Properties command from the Action menu.

Issue certificates for the certificate requests received.

1. Click **Start**, point to **Administrative Tools**, and click **Services**. Make sure that the **Web Publishing** service is enabled.
2. Click **Start**, point to **Administrative Tools**, and then click **Internet Information Services (IIS) Manager**. Make sure that a virtual directory called **certsrv** has been created under the default Web site.
3. Open **Internet Explorer**. In the browser's address bar, type **http://localhost/certsrv/** (**Figure 10-8**).
4. Click the **Request a certificate** link.
5. Click the **Web Browser Certificate** link.
6. In the **Web Browser Certificate Identifying Information**, enter all appropriate information, such as your name and company info (**Figure 10-9**).
7. Click **Submit**. A potential scripting violation may come up. If so, click **Yes** to request a certificate now. This will cause a message to appear in the browser telling you that your request is pending.
8. Make several more requests, following Steps 4-7.

Figure 10-6 CA Properties Window

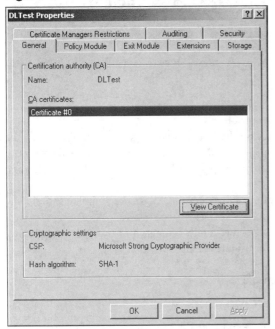

Figure 10-7 Viewing a certificate

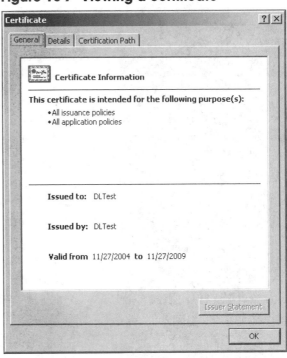

Figure 10-8 Requesting a certificate over the Web

Figure 10-9 Web Browser Certificate – Identifying Information Page

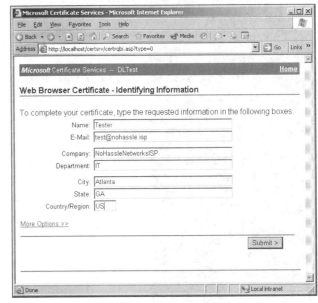

project 10.2

Working with Certificates (cont'd)

exam objective

Basic knowledge

project steps

9. Switch to the **Certification Authority** console.
10. Double-click the server name to display all the folders that the server contains. Click the **Pending Requests** folder in the left pane. All the pending requests for certificates are displayed in the right pane. The right pane displays information related to the pending requests (**Figure 10-10**).
11. Select any request, right-click the request and select the **All Tasks** command to display all the available commands for the request.
12. Click the **Issue** command to accept the certificate request and issue the certificate. The request will move to the **Issued Certificates** folder.
13. Select another request and deny it.
14. Close the **Certification Authority** console.

Renew the certificate of the Standalone root CA.

1. Open the **Certification Authority** console and select the server from the left pane.
2. Right-click the server, select **All Tasks** and click the **Renew CA Certificate** command. A message appears, asking you to stop Certificate Services. Click **Yes**. This will stop the Certificate Services and will open the **Renew CA Certificate** dialog box (**Figure 10-11**).
3. Select the **Yes** option button in the **Renew CA Certificate** dialog box to define a new public and/or private key pair. Select the **No** option button to retain the existing pair of public and private keys.
4. Click **OK** to renew the certificate.
5. Close the **Certification Authority** console. You have now renewed your certificate.

Revoke a certificate issued by the server.

1. Open the **Certification Authority** console.
2. In the left pane, select the server, the Standalone root CA.
3. Double-click the server to display the folders contained in it.
4. Select the **Issued Certificates** folder in the left pane, which displays the certificates issued by the server in the right pane.
5. Select any certificate from the right pane.
6. Right-click the selected certificate, point to **All Tasks** and click the **Revoke Certificate** command to open the **Certificate Revocation** dialog box (**Figure 10-12**).
7. The **Certificate Revocation** dialog box displays a list box containing the reasons for revoking a certificate. Select **Key Compromise** as the reason from the list box to revoke the certificate.
8. Click the **Yes** button to complete the process of revoking the certificate.
9. Close the **Certification Authority** console. You have now revoked a certificate.

Figure 10-10 Pending Requests

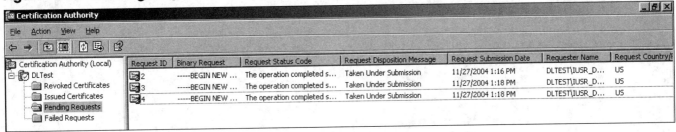

Figure 10-11 Renewing a Certificate

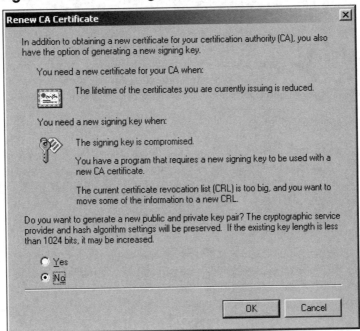

Figure 10-12 Revoking a Certificate

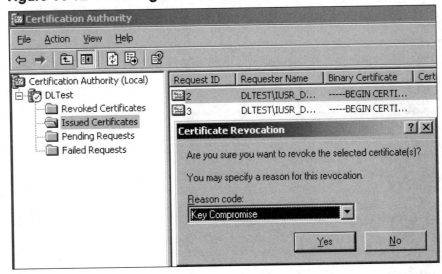

11 Implementing and Managing IP Security

Protecting information while it is in transit across networks is an extremely important component of a network security policy. If not, an attacker may be able to modify file contents or impersonate another computer to gain confidential information. Passwords that are in transit between two computers must also be protected.

There are four fundamental functions of any security system: authentication, confidentiality, integrity, and anti-replay protection. Authentication is the process of verifying that an entity is who or what it claims to be. Confidentiality is the process of ensuring that data is safe from being intercepted, viewed or copied while in transit. Integrity is the process of ensuring that data received is accurate and complete. Anti-replay protection refers to safety measures so that data packets are not retransmitted. Since each datagram sent over a network is unique, it cannot be re-sent, helping to prevent others from intercepting messages and impersonating one of the clients.

In this lesson, we will focus on one of the security features available within Windows Server 2003 that can provide those capabilities: IPSec.

Scenario

You are the network administrator at Dolphin Finance, Inc. Dolphin Finance provides financial consulting services for various clients throughout the United States. The company has 100 employees, with headquarters in Atlanta, Georgia. There is also a branch office in Houston, Texas, with 20 employees. You are responsible for ensuring the security of communications among the users at the Atlanta office. You also need to ensure secure communications between the Atlanta and Texas offices.

Lesson 11 Implementing and Managing IP Security

Project	Exam 70-291 Objective
11.1 Implementing and Configuring IP Security	Monitor network protocol security. Tools might include IP Security Microsoft Management Console (MMC) snap-in and Kerberos support tools. Implement secure network administration procedures.
11.2 Configuring IP Security Filters	Monitor network protocol security. Tools might include IP Security Microsoft Management Console (MMC) snap-in and Kerberos support tools. Implement secure network administration procedures.
11.3 Creating New IP Security Policies and Rules	Monitor network protocol security. Tools might include IP Security Microsoft Management Console (MMC) snap-in and Kerberos support tools. Implement secure network administration procedures.
11.4 Configuring IP Security for Tunneling	Monitor network protocol security. Tools might include IP Security Microsoft Management Console (MMC) snap-in and Kerberos support tools. Implement secure network administration procedures.
11.5 Troubleshooting and Monitoring IP Security Problems	Troubleshoot network protocol security. Tools might include IP Security Monitor MMC snap-in, Event Viewer, and Network Monitor.

General Requirements

To complete the projects in this lesson, you will need administrative rights on a Windows Server 2003 computer. For Project 11.2, you will need administrative rights on an additional Windows Server 2003 computer that is a non-IPSec-enabled DNS server. For Project 11.6, you will need a Windows Server 2003 computer connected to a network with at least one client computer attached. You may also find it helpful to refer to Lesson 11 in your Prentice Hall Certification Series Exam 70-291 textbook for further information on the topics covered by the projects in this lesson.

project 11.1

Implementing and Configuring IP Security

exam objective

Monitor network protocol security. Tools might include IP Security Microsoft Management Console (MMC) snap-in and Kerberos support tools. Implement secure network administration procedures.

overview

Users at the Atlanta office need to communicate with each other, as well as with users at the Texas office. To enable secured communications between users, you need to implement an IPSec policy for the network at the Atlanta office. Additionally, several client representatives visit the Atlanta office frequently and work on certain computers. You need to implement an authentication method using a pre-shared key to ensure that the client representatives do not send or receive unsecured communications.

learning objective

After completing this project, you will know how to configure and implement an IPSec policy on a local computer and add a rule to an IPSec policy to implement an authentication method using a pre-shared key.

specific requirements

To complete this project, you will need administrative rights on a Windows Server 2003 computer.

estimated completion time

20 minutes

project steps

1. Log on to the computer as an **Administrator**.
2. Click **Start**, point to **Administrative Tools**, and then click **Local Security Policy** to open the **Local Security Settings** console. You can access the IPSec policies on your computer from this console.
3. Click the **IP Security Policies On Local Computer** node in the left pane to list the predefined IPSec policies in the right pane.
4. Click the **Server (Request Security)** policy and then click **Assign** on the **Action** menu to implement this policy (or right-click **Server Policy** and select **Assign** from the context menu) **(Figure 11-1)**. The **Policy Assigned** column displays **Yes** for the **Server (Request Security)** policy to indicate that the policy has been implemented on the computer.
5. Click the **Server (Request Security)** policy and then click **Properties** on the **Action** menu to open the **Server (Request Security) Properties** dialog box **(Figure 11-2)**. Using this dialog box, you can modify the properties of the Server (Request Security) policy so that using a pre-shared key is the authentication method.
6. Click **Add** to initiate the **Security Rule Wizard**. The **Welcome** screen of the Security Rule Wizard appears. You use the wizard to change the properties of the policy to add a new rule that authenticates all communications using a pre-shared key.
7. Click **Next** to advance to the **Tunnel Endpoint** screen **(Figure 11-3)**. Using this screen, you can specify the details for using IPSec tunnels. Accept the default selection, **This rule does not specify a tunnel**.
8. Click **Next** to advance to the **Network Type** screen **(Figure 11-4)**. Here, you can specify the type of network for applying the policy.
9. Accept the default selection, **All network connections** and then click **Next** to advance to the **IP Filters List** screen **(Figure 11-5)**.

Figure 11-1 Assigning the Server (Request Security) Policy

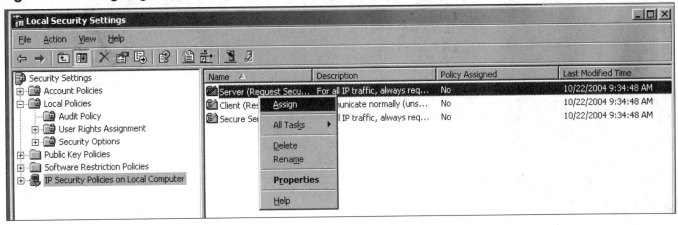

Figure 11-2 Server (Request Security) Properties dialog box

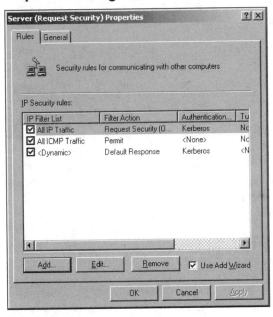

Figure 11-3 Tunnel EndPoint screen

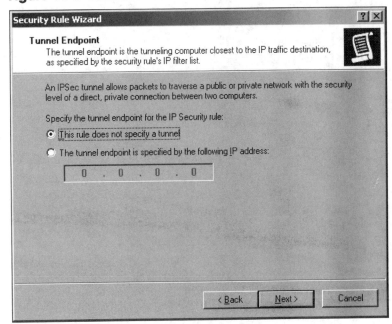

Figure 11-4 Network Type screen

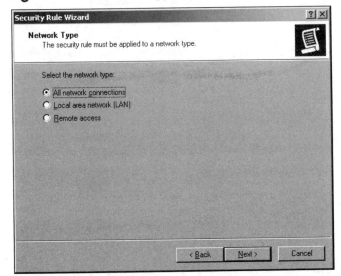

Figure 11-5 IP Filter List screen

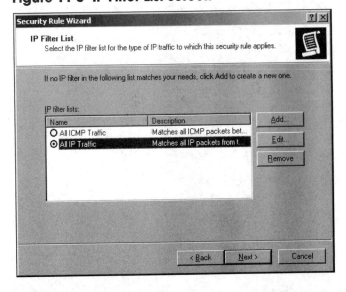

project 11.1

Implementing and Configuring
IP Security (cont'd)

exam objective

Monitor network protocol security. Tools might include IP Security Microsoft Management Console (MMC) snap-in and Kerberos support tools. Implement secure network administration procedures.

project steps

10. Click the **All IP Traffic** option button and click **Next** to advance to the **Filter Action** screen (**Figure 11-6**).
11. Click **Add** to add a new (custom) Filter Action. This will launch the **IP Security Filter Action Wizard**.
12. Click **Next** to bypass the Wizard Welcome Screen and go directly to the **Filter Action Name** screen (**Figure 11-7**).
13. Type **Force Security**, then click **Next**. The **Filter Action General Options** screen appears (**Figure 11-8**).
14. Accept the default, **Negotiate Security** and click **Next**. The Wizard will then prompt you concerning computers that don't support IPSec.
15. Accept the default, **Do not communicate with computers that do not support IPSec**, and click **Next**. The **IP Traffic Security** screen appears.
16. Select the **Custom** option button and click **Settings** to display the **Custom Security Method Settings** dialog box (**Figure 11-9**).
17. Note the different options available. For Data integrity, there are two choices: MD5 or SHA1. For Data Encryption, you have the choice between DES and Triple DES (3DES). Also note that you can control how often to generate new session keys (per so many kilobytes or per so many seconds).
18. Click **OK** to close the Custom Security Method Settings dialog box.
19. Click **Finish** to close the IP Security Filter Action Wizard. This takes you back to the Filter Action screen (**Figure 11-10**).
20. Select the new rule you just created and click **Next**. This opens the **Authentication Method** screen. Using this screen, you can specify the authentication method to be used for authenticating IP packets.
21. Click the **Use this string to protect the key exchange (preshared key)** option button to specify that a pre-shared key be used for authentication. Type **Mykey** in the **Use this string to protect the key exchange (preshared key)** text box (**Figure 11-11**).
22. Click **Next** to advance to the **Completing the Security Rule Wizard** screen.
23. Click **Finish** on the Completing the Security Rule Wizard screen.
24. This will return you to the Properties dialog box for the Server Policy. Click **OK**.
25. Close the Local Security Settings console. You have configured a policy on the server to use a pre-shared key as the authentication method for IP packets policy.

Figure 11-6 Filter Action screen

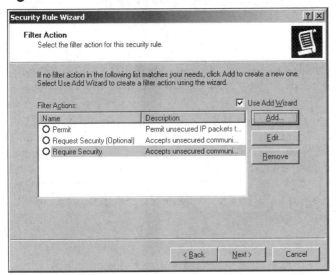

Figure 11-7 Filter Action Name screen

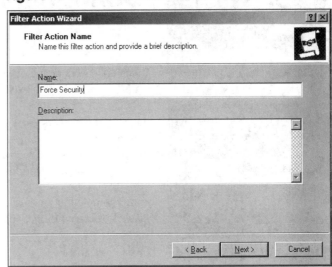

Figure 11-8 Filter Action General Options screen

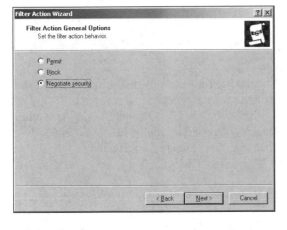

Figure 11-9 Custom Security Method Settings

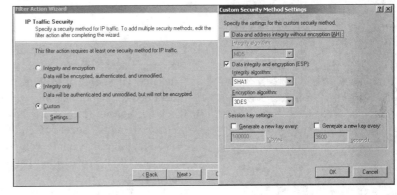

Figure 11-10 Filter Action screen—Custom Filter Added

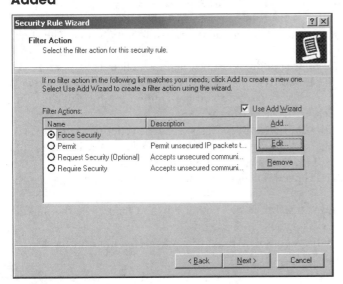

Figure 11-11 Authentication Method screen

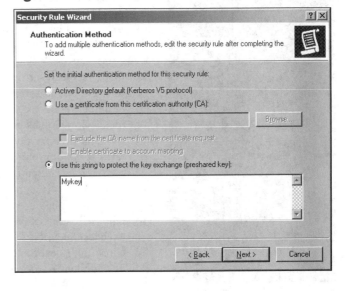

project 11.2

Configuring IP Security Filters

exam objective

Monitor network protocol security. Tools might include IP Security Microsoft Management Console (MMC) snap-in and Kerberos support tools. Implement secure network administration procedures.

overview

One of the servers on your network is a non-IPSec enabled DNS server (Server2). It communicates with computers configured with different Windows versions, such as Windows 98 and Windows NT. You need to configure all the other computers on your network to be able to identify communications from this server.

learning objective

After completing this project, you will know how to configure an IPSec filter to identify IP packets received from a specific computer.

specific requirements

To complete and test this project, you will need administrative rights on two Windows Server 2003 computers (Server1 and Server2). Server2 should be a non-IPSec-enabled DNS server. The project also can be completed setting a source IP to destination IP filter using a single server if you do not wish to test the results.

estimated completion time

15 minutes

project steps

1. Log on to **Server2** as an **Administrator**.
2. Open the **Local Security Settings** console.
3. Click the **IP Security Policies On Local Machine** node in the left pane to list the predefined IPSec policies on your computer in the right pane of the console.
4. Click the **Server (Request Security)** policy and then click **Properties** on the **Action** menu to open the **Server (Request Security) Properties** dialog box. This dialog box lists all the filter lists on the computer that you can configure for this policy.
5. Click the **All IP Traffic** filter list in the **IP Security Rules** list box to select the filter list that you want to configure.
6. Click the **Edit** button to open the **Edit Rule Properties** dialog box. You can use this dialog box to change the property of a filter.
7. Select the **All IP Traffic** filter list option button to specify that you will configure the All IP Traffic filter list, which is used to check if the IP packets match the properties specified in the filter (**Figure 11-12**).
8. Click the **Edit** button to open the **IP Filter List** dialog box (**Figure 11-13**). This dialog box lists all the filters available in the All IP Traffic filter list.
9. Select the filter in the list and click the **Edit** button to open the **Filter Properties** dialog box. You can specify the source and destination addresses of the two communicating computers using this dialog box.
10. Click the down-arrow in the **Source address** list box and then click the **A specific IP address** option to enable the **IP Address** text box. Specify the IP address of Server2 (**Figure 11-14**) as the source address because you are configuring the filter list for identifying IP packets that Server1 receives from Server2.
11. Click the down arrow in the **Destination address** list box and then click the **A specific IP address** option button to enable the **IP Address** text box. Specify the IP address of Server1, the computer that will receive communications from Server2.
12. Click **OK** to close the **Filter Properties** dialog box and then click **Close** to close the IP Filter List dialog box.
13. Click **Close** to close the Edit Rule Properties dialog box and then close the Server (Request Security) Properties dialog box.
14. Close the Local Security Settings console. You have configured a filter for the All IP Traffic filter list of the Server (Request Security) policy.

Figure 11-12 IP Traffic filter list

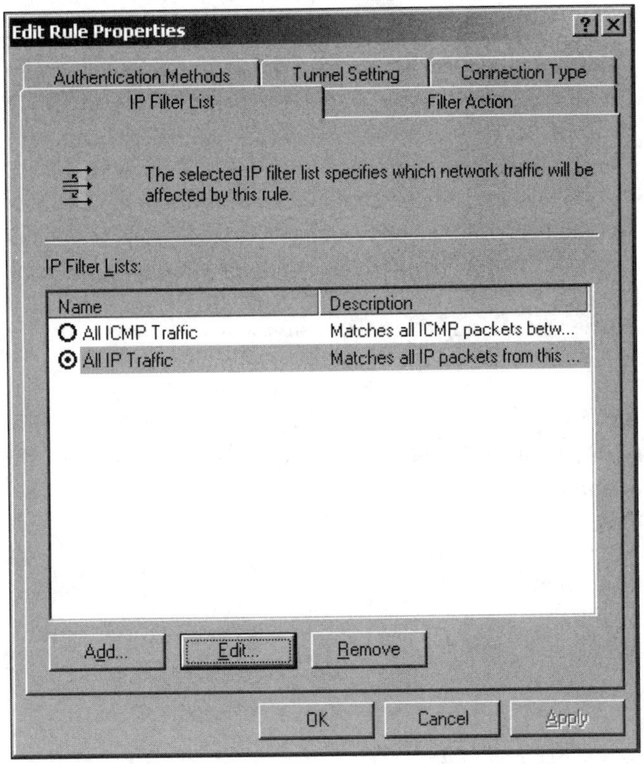

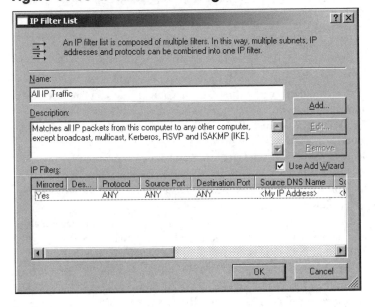

Figure 11-13 IP Filter List dialog box

Figure 11-14 IP Filter Properties dialog box

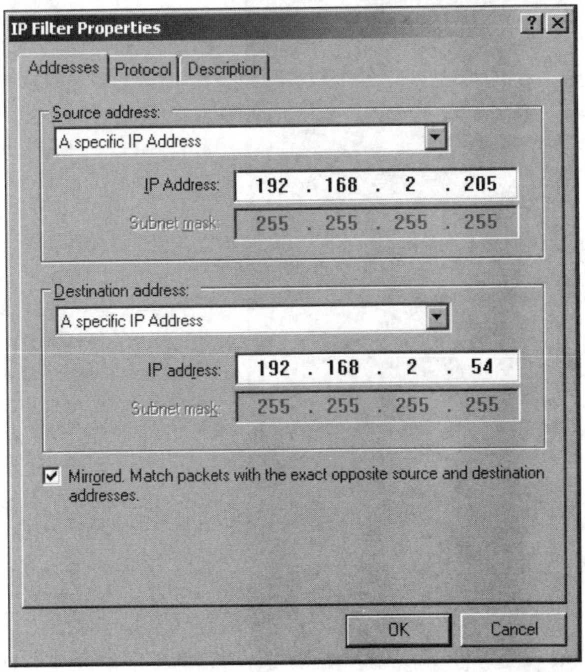

Creating New IP Security Policies and Rules

exam objective

Monitor network protocol security. Tools might include IP Security Microsoft Management Console (MMC) snap-in and Kerberos support tools. Implement secure network administration procedures.

overview

Clients visiting your office need to communicate with remote users who may not have IPSec enabled on their computers. Therefore, you need to create a new IPSec policy on one of the computers on your network to allow communication with remote, non-IPSec enabled computers. Additionally, you need to ensure that communications between this computer and all other computers on the local network are secure.

learning objective

After completing this project, you will know how to create a new IPSec policy.

specific requirements

To complete this project, you will need administrative rights on a Windows Server 2003 computer.

estimated completion time

10 minutes

project steps

1. Log on to the computer as an **Administrator**.
2. Open the **Local Security Settings** console. You can create new IPSec policies on a computer using this console.
3. Click **IP Security Policy On Local Computer** in the left pane of the Local Security Settings console to list the IPSec policies on your computer in the right pane.
4. Open the **Action** menu and then click **Create IP Security Policy** to initiate the **IP Security Policy Wizard**. The **Welcome** screen of the IP Security Policy Wizard appears. This Wizard enables you to create a new IPSec policy.
5. Click **Next** to open the **IP Security Policy Name** screen. Type a name to specify a name for the new policy (**Figure 11-15**).
6. Click **Next** to open the **Requests For Secure Communication** screen. This screen will enable you to specify how your computer will handle requests for secure communications from other computers.
7. Accept the default selection, **Activate the default response rule** check box to add this rule to your policy. You need to add this rule to your policy to provide secure communications to other computers when they make such a request (**Figure 11-16**).
8. Click **Next** to open the **Default Response Rule Authentication method** screen. Using this screen, you can specify an authentication method for the policy.
9. Accept the default selection, **Windows 2003 default (Kerberos V5 protocol)**, to specify the Kerberos V5 protocol as the initial authentication method for the response rule.
10. Click **Next** to open the **Completing the New Rule Wizard** screen of the wizard. The screen states that the policy has been created successfully.
11. Click **Finish** to complete the creation of an IPSec policy. The *<Policy_Name>* **Properties** dialog box appears automatically to enable you to specify additional properties for the new policy. It also lists the default filter lists available for the policy on the computer.
12. Click **OK** to close the Properties dialog box, as you do not need to specify any further properties for the policy.
13. The **Local Security Settings** console appears again, listing the new IPSec policy, along with the predefined policies.
14. Close the Local Security Settings console. This completes the creation of an IPSec policy on the computer. The new policy will enable your computer to connect to external remote computers as well as provide secure communications to the local computers.

Figure 11-15 IP Security Policy Name screen

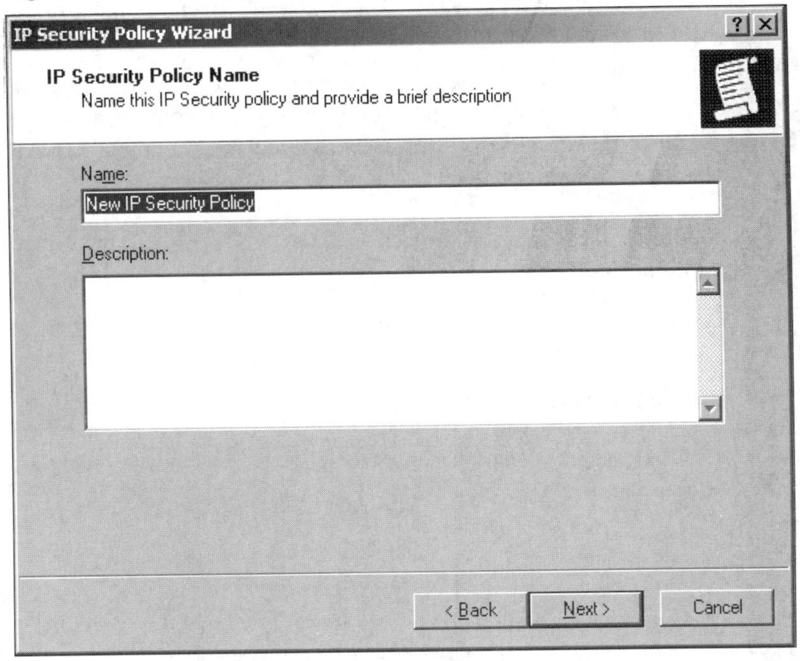

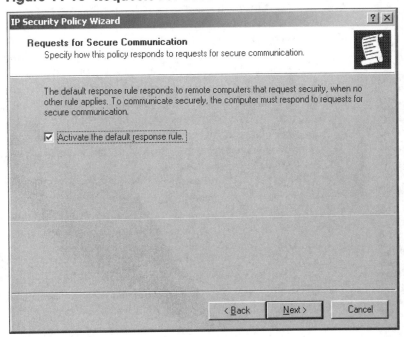

Figure 11-16 Requests For Secure Communication screen

project 11.4

Configuring IP Security for Tunneling

exam objective

Monitor network protocol security. Tools might include IP Security Microsoft Management Console (MMC) snap-in and Kerberos support tools. Implement secure network administration procedures.

overview

The computers at the Atlanta office are configured to communicate with the computers at the Texas office through the Internet. However, as communication over the Internet is not secure, you need to ensure secure data transfer between the computers at the two offices by providing a secure connection between the servers at the sites.

learning objective

After completing this project, you will know how to create an IPSec tunnel to a remote computer.

specific requirements

To complete and test this project, you will need administrative rights on two Windows Server 2003 computers (Server1 and Server2).

estimated completion time

20 minutes

project steps

1. Log on to the first computer (**Server1**) as an **Administrator**.
2. Open the **Local Security Settings** console.
3. Click **IP Security Policy On Local Computer** in the left pane of the Local Security Settings console, open the **Action** menu, and then click **Create IP Security Policy** to initiate the **IP Security Policy Wizard**. The **Welcome** screen of the IP Security Policy Wizard appears. Using this wizard, you can configure an IPSec policy to create an IPSec tunnel to another computer.
4. Click **Next** to open the **IP Security Policy Name** screen of the wizard.
5. Type a name to specify the policy name of the IPSec tunnel.
6. Provide a description for the policy that you are creating in the **Description** text box (**Figure 11-17**).
7. Click **Next** to open the **Requests For Secure Communication** screen. The Requests for Secure Communication screen of the wizard enables you to specify how your computer will handle requests for secure communications from other computers.
8. Clear the **Activate Default Response Rule** check box to disable the default response rule for this policy. The default response rule responds to secured communications requests from other computers when no other rules are available. Since you are communicating with only one computer in this procedure, and will use a tunnel rule, you do not need to specify the default response rule.
9. Click **Next** to open the **Completing the IP Security Wizard** screen. This screen informs you of the successful creation of the policy.
10. Click **Finish** to complete the creation of the IPSec policy. The **<Policy_Name> Properties** dialog box appears, enabling you to create a tunnel rule for the policy.
11. Click **Add** on the **Rules** tab of the dialog box to initiate the **Security Rule Wizard**. You can configure the IPSec policy to include a tunnel rule using this Wizard. The **Welcome** screen of the IP Security Policy Wizard appears and provides information about rules.
12. Click **Next** to open the **Tunnel Endpoint** screen. The Tunnel Endpoint screen enables you to specify the computer that will form the other end of the tunnel Server2.

Figure 11-17 Naming an IPSec rule

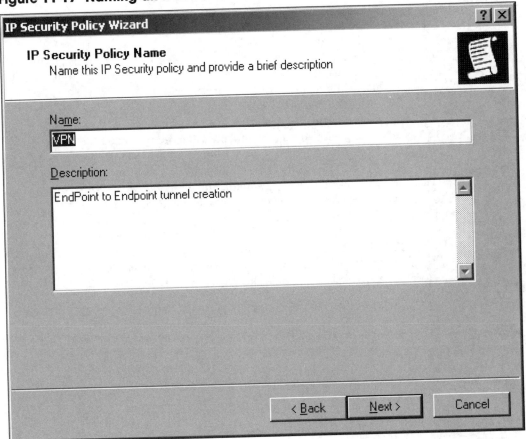

project 11.4

Configuring IP Security for Tunneling *(cont'd)*

exam objective

Monitor network protocol security. Tools might include IP Security Microsoft Management Console (MMC) snap-in and Kerberos support tools. Implement secure network administration procedures.

project steps

13. Click the option button labeled **The tunnel endpoint is specified by this IP address** to display the **IP address** dialog box. Specify the IP address of the computer that forms the other end of the tunnel (**Figure 11-18**).

14. Click **Next** to open the **Network Type** screen. The Network Type screen enables you to specify the type of network connection this rule should be for.

15. Click the **Local Area Network (LAN)** option button to specify a LAN type connection for the tunnel.

16. Click **Next** to open the **IP Filter List** screen. Using this screen, you can add a filter list to the policy.

17. Click the **All IP Traffic** option button in the IP filter lists list to add a filter list that will apply the rule to all IP packets.

18. Click **Next** to open the **Filter Action** screen. Here, you can specify how the policy will handle the IP packets if the IP address of the policy matches the IP address of computer that will form the other end of the tunnel.

19. Click the **Require Security** option button to specify that filter action will allow only secure communications from the computer.

20. Click **Next** to open the **Authentication Method** screen.

21. Accept the default selection, **Windows 2003 Default (Kerberos V5 Protocol)**, to specify the Kerberos protocol as the authentication method for the policy.

22. Click **Next** to open the **Completing the IP Security Wizard** screen. This screen informs you of the successful creation of the rule for the policy.

23. Click **Finish** to close the Security Rule Wizard.

24. Click **Close** to close the *<Policy_Name>* Properties dialog box.

25. Close the Local Security Settings console. This completes the creation of an IPSec policy to start an IPSec tunnel. Similarly, you need to create and configure an IPSec policy on the computer that forms the tunnel endpoint.

Figure 11-18 Specifying an IPSec Tunnel Endpoint

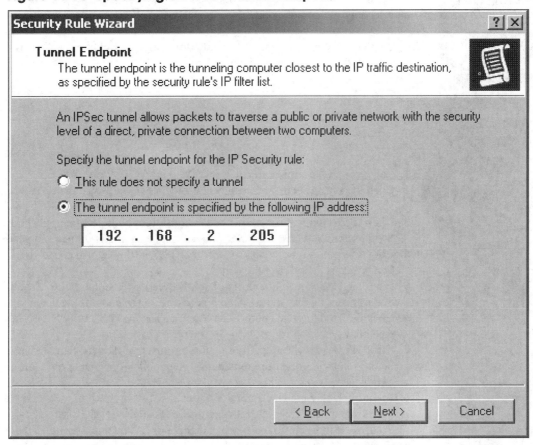

project 11.5

Troubleshooting and Monitoring IP Security Problems

exam objective

Troubleshoot network protocol security. Tools might include IP Security Monitor MMC snap-in, Event Viewer, and Network Monitor.

overview

The IPSec policy you just created is facing some integrity problems when responding to requests from computers with secure communications. Therefore, you need to delete this policy and restore the default policies provided by Windows Server 2003 on the computer. After restoring the default policies, you should test the communications between the computers to see if they are secure.

learning objective

After completing this project, you will know how to delete a policy from a computer, restore the default Windows Server 2003 policies on a computer, and use Netsh to view communication between two computers that implement IPSec Policies.

specific requirements

To complete this project, you will need administrative rights on a Windows Server 2003 computer, and successful completion of Project 14.3.

estimated completion time

15 minutes

project steps

1. Log on as an **Administrator** to **Server1**.
2. Open the **Local Security Settings** console on Server1. You can use this console to manage IPSec policies on the computer.
3. Click **IP Security Policy On Local Computer** in the left pane of the Local Security Settings console to list the IPSec policies on the computer in the right pane.
4. Click the policy you created in Project 14.3 in the right pane of the Local Security Settings console to select the policy.
5. Open the **Action** menu and then click **Delete** to delete the policy. The Local Security Settings console displays a dialog box asking you to confirm the deletion.
6. Click the **Yes** button to confirm the deletion. The Local Security Settings console deletes the policy.
7. Click **IP Security Policy On Local Computer** in the left pane of the Local Security Settings console to list the remaining IPSec policies available on your computer in the right pane.
8. Right-click **IP Security Policy On Local Computer**. Click **All Tasks** to display the **Tasks** menu, and then select **Restore Default Policies (Figure 11-19)**. The Local Security Settings console displays a dialog box asking you to confirm the restoration.
9. Click the **Yes** button to confirm the restoration of the default policies. The Local Security Settings console restores all the default policies provided by the Windows Server 2003 operating system. You can now test the communication line between Server1 and another computer.
10. Close the Local Securities Settings console and then open the **Run** dialog box on Server1.
11. Type **cmd** in the **Open** text box and click **OK** to open the **Command Prompt** window **(Figure 11-20)**.
12. Type **Netsh** and press **[Enter]**. Then type **ipsec static** and press **[Enter]**. Then type **show policy all normal** and press **[Enter]** to show the list of policies.
13. Type **dynamic** and press **[Enter]**. Then type **show mmsas all** and press **[Enter]** to display the main mode authentication associations.
14. Close the Command Prompt window and the IP Security Monitor window.

Figure 11-19 Restore Default Policies

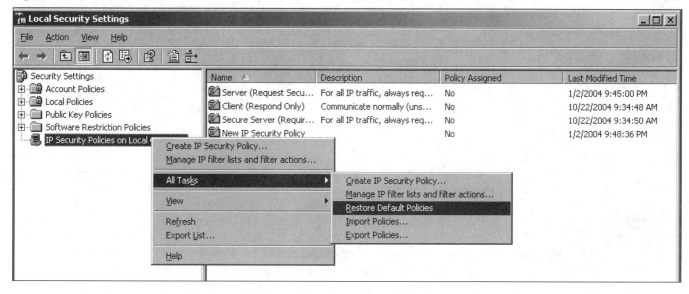

Figure 11-20 Netsh IPSec

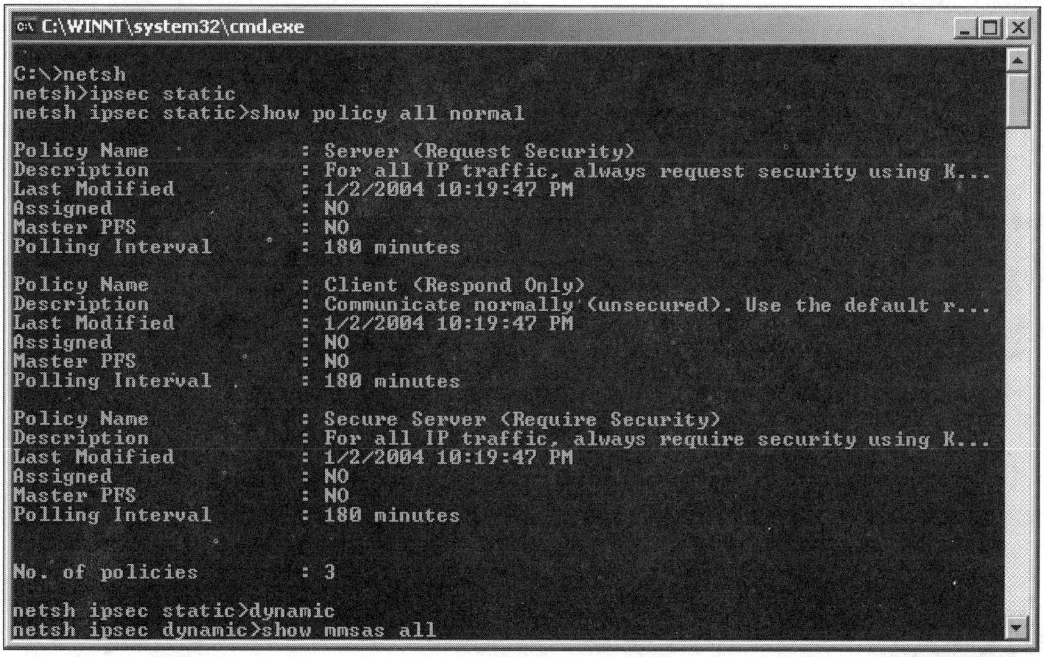

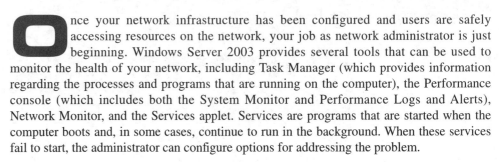

LESSON 12

Maintaining a Windows Server 2003 Network Infrastructure

Once your network infrastructure has been configured and users are safely accessing resources on the network, your job as network administrator is just beginning. Windows Server 2003 provides several tools that can be used to monitor the health of your network, including Task Manager (which provides information regarding the processes and programs that are running on the computer), the Performance console (which includes both the System Monitor and Performance Logs and Alerts), Network Monitor, and the Services applet. Services are programs that are started when the computer boots and, in some cases, continue to run in the background. When these services fail to start, the administrator can configure options for addressing the problem.

This lesson includes projects that will enable you to practice using all of these tools.

Scenario

As the network engineer for UnRealistic Expectations, Inc. (a bearish stock market analyst firm), you are responsible for ensuring the smooth operation of the new Windows Server 2003 network. As part of these duties you will diagnose and troubleshoot network and network-related service issues.

Lesson 12　Maintaining a Windows Server 2003 Network Infrastructure

Project	Exam 70-291 Objective
12.1 Monitoring Network Traffic Using Task Manager	Monitor network traffic. Tools might include Network Monitor and System Monitor.
12.2 Monitoring Network Traffic Using Performance Console	Monitor network traffic. Tools might include Network Monitor and System Monitor.
12.3 Monitoring Network Traffic Using Network Monitor	Monitor network traffic. Tools might include Network Monitor and System Monitor.
12.4 Troubleshooting Server Services	Troubleshoot server services. Diagnose and resolve issues related to service dependency. Use service recovery options to diagnose and resolve service-related issues.

General Requirements

To complete the projects in this lesson, you will need administrative rights on a Windows Server 2003 computer. You may also find it helpful to refer to Lesson 12 in your Prentice Hall Certification Series Exam 70-291 textbook for further information on the topics covered by the projects in this lesson.

project 12.1	# Monitoring Network Traffic Using Task Manager
exam objective	Monitor network traffic. Tools might include Network Monitor and System Monitor.
overview	The UnRealistic technology stock analyst department reports significant slowdowns accessing its new Windows Server 2003 computer. You need to get a quick overview of the network traffic that this computer sees.
learning objective	After completing this project, you will know how to use Task Manager to quickly survey the networking situation from the perspective of one server.
specific requirements	See general requirements.
estimated completion time	10 minutes
project steps	1. Log on as an **Administrator**. 2. Open **Task Manager** by pressing **[Ctrl]+[Alt]+[Delete]** and then clicking the **Task Manager** button. 3. Click the **Networking** tab. 4. Examine the network utilization as a whole by looking at the graph (**Figure 12-1**). 5. Open the **View** menu and click **Select Columns**. 6. Check the check boxes as shown in **Figure 12-1**, and click **OK**. 7. Examine the number of Non-Unicasts sent and received. If these are larger than 20% of the Unicasts sent and received, respectively, then a broadcast or multicast storm could be causing excess traffic.

Figure 12-1 Networking tab in the Task Manager and Select Columns dialog box

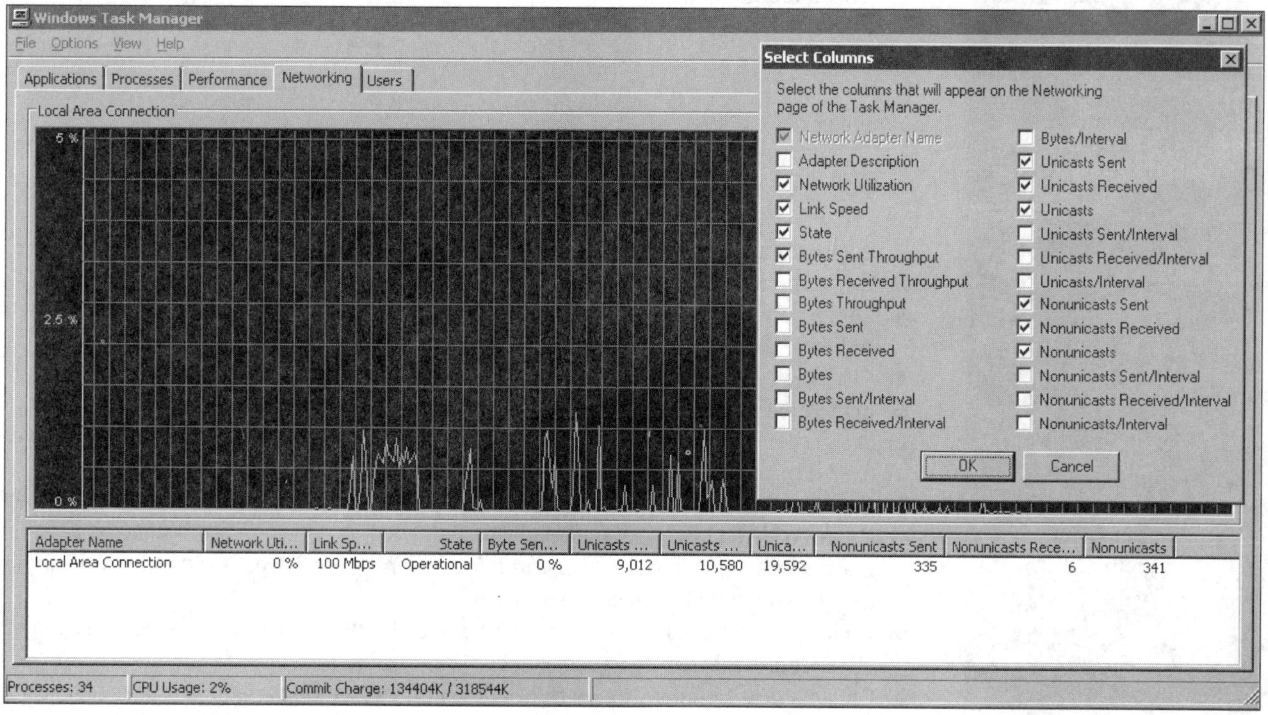

<table>
<tr><td>

project 12.2

</td><td>

Monitoring Network Traffic Using Performance Console

</td></tr>
<tr><td>

exam objective

</td><td>

Monitor Network Traffic. Tools might include Network Monitor and System Monitor.

</td></tr>
<tr><td>

overview

</td><td>

You are receiving complaints from the analysts that they are experiencing intermittent slow-downs when attempting to access the investment banking division's CRM server. Consequently, they cannot learn which companies are using UnRealistic Expectations to underwrite stock and bond offerings, making it more difficult for them to know how to write their analyses.

</td></tr>
<tr><td>

learning objective

</td><td>

After completing this project, you will know how to use the Performance console to help you track down intermittent problems.

</td></tr>
<tr><td>

specific requirements

</td><td>

See general requirements.

</td></tr>
<tr><td>

estimated completion time

</td><td>

15 minutes

</td></tr>
<tr><td>

project steps

</td><td>

1. Log on as an **Administrator**.
2. Click **Start**, point to **Administrative Tools**, and then click **Performance**.
3. Remove the three existing counters by clicking each of the counters listed at the bottom and then clicking the **Delete** button or pressing **[Delete]**.
4. Click the **Add** button.
5. In the **Performance Object** drop-down list, select **Network Interface**.
6. Select the **All Counters** option button and click **Add (Figure 12-2)**. Click **Close** to close the Add Counters dialog box.
7. Examine the graph. This provides an excellent way to see Unicasts and Non-Unicasts as a portion of the total sent and received.
8. Because the slowdowns are intermittent, you may not encounter the difficulties in real time so you will need to set up a log.
9. Click the plus sign to the left of **Performance Logs and Alerts** in the left pane, and then click **Counter Logs**.
10. Create a new Counter Log by right-clicking **Counter Logs** in the left pane and selecting **New Log Settings (Figure 12-3)**.
11. In the **New Log Settings** dialog box, enter **Network Issues** in the **Name** text box, and then click **OK** to open the **Network Issues** dialog box **(Figure 12-4)**.
12. Click the **Add Objects** button in the Network Issues dialog box to open the **Add Objects** dialog box.
13. Select **Network Interface** and click the **Add** button. Then click **Close**.
14. Click the **Schedule** tab in the **Network Issues** dialog box.
15. Select the **After** option in the **Stop log** section and enter **5**. In the **Units** box, select **hours** **(Figure 12-5)**.
16. Accept the remaining defaults by clicking **OK**.
17. If prompted to create a folder for the Performance Log files, click **Yes**.
18. You should see the new Counter Logs icon in the right pane and it should be colored green to indicate that it is actively logging.
19. You would then be able to view this log later to identify the intermittent issues.

</td></tr>
</table>

tip

When monitoring network issues and writing to the log, write the log to local disk, so as to prevent additional network traffic.

Figure 12-2 Add Counters dialog box

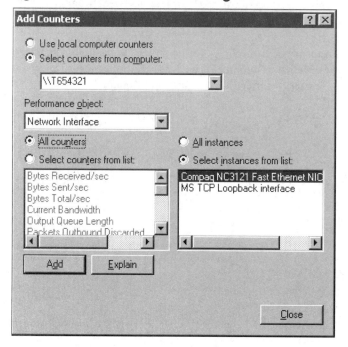

Figure 12-3 New Log Settings command

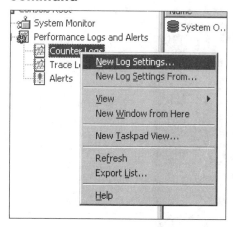

Figure 12-4 General tab in the Network Issues dialog box

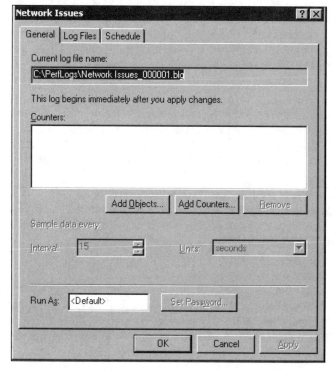

Figure 12-5 Schedule tab in the Network Issues dialog box

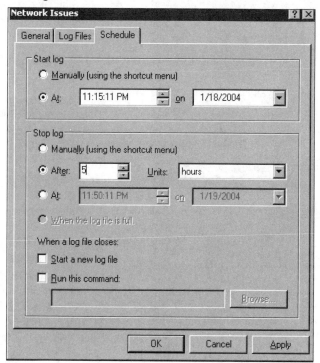

project 12.3

Monitoring Network Traffic Using Network Monitor

exam objective

Monitor Network Traffic. Tools might include Network Monitor and System Monitor.

overview

From your research using the Performance Console, you have noticed that a high percentage of the packets and even bytes received are Non-unicast packets. To further investigate, you need to use a protocol analyzer (or packet sniffer) such as Network Monitor.

learning objective

After completing this project, you will know how to use Network Monitor to decipher network problems.

specific requirements

Administrative rights on a Windows Server 20003 computer with Network Monitor installed.

estimated completion time

20 minutes

project steps

1. Log on as an **Administrator**.
2. Click **Start**, point to **Administrative Tools**, and then click **Network Monitor** to open **Network Monitor**.
3. Since you suspect broadcast traffic to be the problem, you will configure a filter to capture only incoming broadcasts. Click **Capture** on the Menu bar, and click **Filters**.
4. Click the address pairs and then click the **Address** button to open the **Address Expression** dialog box **(Figure 12-6)**.
5. Select the **Include** option button. In the **Station 1** list box, select **ANY GROUP**. In the **Station 2** list box, select **BROADCAST**. In the **Direction** box, select →. Then click **OK**.
6. To begin capturing, click **Capture** on the Menu bar and click **Start**. Simulate some broadcast traffic by opening a **Command Prompt** window and typing **ping 1.1.1.1**.
7. Switch back to Network Monitor and stop capturing by clicking **Capture** on the Menu bar and then clicking **Stop**.
8. Observe the count of broadcasts in the **Network Statistics** frame. Also note that the lower frame reveals the different network addresses and summarizes their traffic that was captured. From here you can see which addresses are generating the most broadcasts. Note which address sent the most broadcasts.
9. Click **Capture** on the Menu bar and then click **Display Captured Data** to display the captured packets.
10. Observe the different types of broadcast traffic and their sources **(Figure 12-7)**.
11. Examine some of the traffic from the most prolific broadcaster (noted in Step10), by double-clicking on one of its packets. This will display the detail frame **(Figure 12-8)**.
12. Click the plus sign to the left of **ETHERNET**.
13. Click **ETHERNET: Source address**. Observe how it highlights certain sets of hex digits in the Hexadecimal frame below.
14. Create a display filter so that only traffic from this computer is displayed, by right-clicking **ETHERNET: Source address** and then clicking **Add to Filter (Figure 12-9)**. This will display the **Property** tab of the **Expression** dialog box **(Figure 12-10)**.
15. Click **OK**. In the **Display Filter** dialog box, click **OK** again. Now you can analyze the broadcast packets (what you captured) from the most prolific broadcaster (what you filtered in your display).

Figure 12-7 Viewing Captured Data

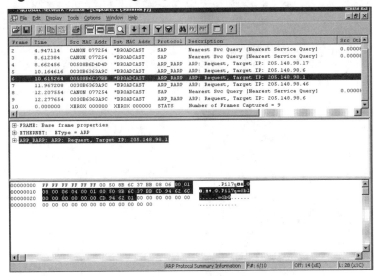

Figure 12-6 Configuring an Address Filter

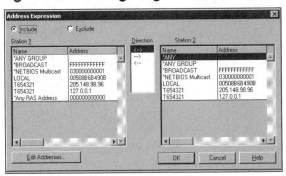

Figure 12-8 Ethernet Source Address

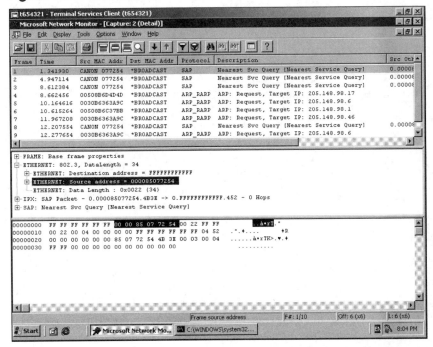

Figure 12-9 Adding to a Filter (the fast way)

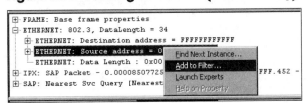

Figure 12-10 The Property tab in the Expression dialog box

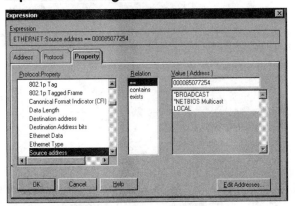

project 12.4

Troubleshooting Server Services

exam objective

Troubleshoot server services. Diagnose and resolve issues related to service dependency. Use service recovery options to diagnose and resolve service-related issues.

overview

In attempting to make the Windows Server 2003 computer that serves as your firewall more secure, you decide to disable a number of services (among them the Remote Access Connection Manager Service).

learning objective

After completing this project, you will know how to use the dependency information available in the Services applet to troubleshoot problems with network services.

specific requirements

See general requirements.

estimated completion time

15 minutes

project steps

1. Log on as an **Administrator**.
2. Click **Start**, point to **Administrative Tools**, and then click **Services**.
3. Ensure that the **Internet Connection Firewall (ICF)/Internet Connection Sharing (ICS) Service** is enabled but stopped.
4. Disable the **Remote Access Connection Manager** and ensure that it is stopped.
5. Then simulate a reboot by starting the **Internet Connection Firewall (ICF)/Internet Connection Sharing (ICS) Service**. This will fail and a message box notifying you of this will appear **(Figure 12-11)**.
6. Open the **Properties** dialog box for the **Internet Connection Firewall (ICF)/Internet Connection Sharing (ICS) Service** and click the **Dependencies** tab **(Figure 12-12)**.
7. Check the status of each of the services upon which ICF/ICS depends.
8. When you find the service that was not started or would not start, ensure that it is enabled and try to start it.
9. Examine Event Viewer and the System Log to see how you could have more quickly pinpointed the issue **(Figure 12-13)**. Note that the message explains which of the dependent services caused the problem.

tip

The Event Viewer is an excellent source of information when troubleshooting services.

Figure 12-11 Error Message—Service won't start

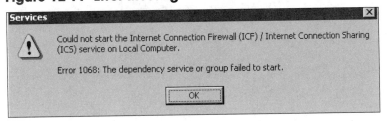

Figure 12-12 Service Dependencies

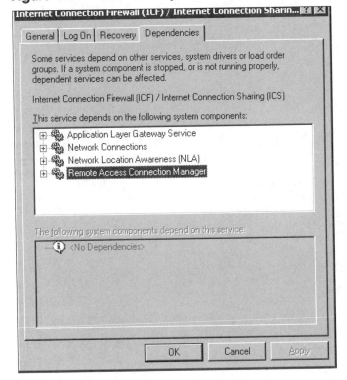

Figure 12-13 Event description in Event Properties dialog box

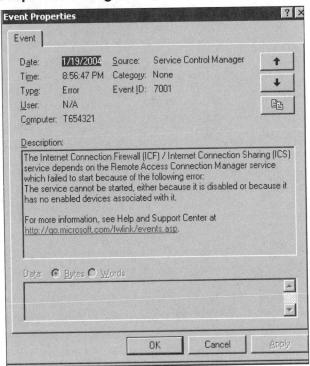

Glossary

Active Directory-integrated zone A DNS zone that stores DNS information in Active Directory.

Address (A) record A resource record that associates a host name to the host's IP address.

Address Resolution Protocol (ARP) A protocol responsible for resolving IP addresses to hardware (MAC) addresses on the local subnet.

Alias A nickname for a computer name that is mapped to an IP address.

Alert logs A tool that allows Administrators to configure System Monitor to watch specific counters and then perform an action when a specific value has been reached.

AppleTalk LAN architecture built into Apple Macintosh computers and laser printers used to interact with the OSI model.

Application layer Located at the top of the TCP/IP protocol stack, the Application layer enables applications to access the services of the other layers and defines the protocols that applications must use to exchange data.

Application Program Interface (API) Generic code that permits application programmers to program application code to call functions such as network functions.

ANDing An operation that is performed by multiplying one binary number by another binary number resulting in the network address for a given IP address. ANDing is also referred to as the logical AND operation.

ARP cache A storage area that maintains a temporary record of mappings of IP addresses to hardware addresses.

ARP utility Utility used to display and modify the IP address-to-physical address (MAC address) translation tables used by the Address Resolution Protocol.

Audit logging The process by which a DHCP server maintains a record of its activities in a text file; serves as a troubleshooting tool.

Authentication The process of verifying that an entity is who or what it claims to be.

Authentication Header (AH) A protocol that ensures authentication and message integrity for transmitted packets.

Authentication Method Determines the method used to authenticate the entities involved.

Authorization The process that determines what the user is permitted to do on the system or network.

Automatic Private IP Addressing (APIPA) Feature of Windows Server 2003 that computers use to assign themselves an IP address automatically when a DHCP server is not available.

Baseline Data that represents the normal performance of a server such as a DNS server.

Bootstrap Protocol (BOOTP) A protocol that enables diskless clients to configure TCP/IP automatically and thereby obtain IP addresses.

Border Gateway Protocol (BGP) An exterior routing protocol used to exchange information between networks that are administered under different administrative authorities.

Broadcast A method of NetBIOS name resolution that sends requests simultaneously to all network hosts.

Caching A method of storing frequently used information in memory so that it can be accessed quickly when required.

Caching-only name server A DNS server that does not have its own local zone database file.

Certificate A digital document that is used for authentication and to secure information. It binds a public key to the user/computer/service that holds the private key.

Certificate Revocation List A document maintained and published by a CA. It lists revoked certificates.

Certification Authorities Entities that issue, manage, and vouch for the authenticity of the public keys they issue to users/computers/services. They also can vouch for other CAs.

Certification Services A Windows Server 2003 service that issues certificates for a particular CA. Installing this service allows a server to perform the role of a Certificate Authority in a Public Key Infrastructure.

Classless Inter-Domain Routing (CIDR) A method of subnetting that removes the requirement that all subnets be of equal size and provides an easy way of notating subnet masks. In CIDR, the class of address you are given does not necessarily denote the network section of an address.

Client (Respond Only) A default IPSec policy under which computers will never initiate a request to use IPSec for data transmission but will enter a negotiation with Internet Key Exchange when requested to do so by another computer.

Confidentiality The process of ensuring that data is safe from being intercepted, viewed, or copied while in transit.

Counter Represents a characteristic of an object that can be measured.

Counter logs A tool that is used to collect information from counters that monitor how hardware is used, as well as system services.

Cryptography The process of keeping information secure.

Default gateway A router that links networks and manages the information needed to do so, enabling client hosts to get data to or from a computer outside the local subnet. A client host identifies whatever router that is on its own subnet as its default gateway.

Delegated zones Zones created to manage portions of the chain of domains using contiguous names.

Demand-dial interface Helps a Windows Server 2003 computer establish a connection with a remote router on another network.

Demand-dial routing Cost-saving method of connecting to a remote network only for the time during which the connection is required.

DHCPAcknowledgment Message packet sent by the DHCP server to the client that verifies that the client can use the IP address that was offered.

DHCPDiscover Message packet that DHCP clients broadcast to locate a DHCP server on the network.

DHCPOffer Message packet the DHCP server sends to the DHCP client to offer an available IP address.

DHCPRequest Message packet sent by the DHCP client to the DHCP server to request use of the IP address that has been offered.

DHCP Relay Agent A routing protocol that makes it possible for DHCP clients to request an IP address from a DHCP server that is located on a remote subnet. Without a relay agent, broadcast packets cannot travel through routers.

Digital Signature Provides a way for an entity that sends a file, message, or other digital information to bind its identity to the information being sent.

DNS namespace The hierarchical arrangement of domains in DNS.

DNS server A server that maintains a DNS database for the purpose of resolving host names to IP addresses.

Domain name A name of an IP host such as prenhall.com that is used in place of an IP address.

Domain Name System (DNS) A naming system service that is used to locate IP-based computers by translating their fully qualified domain names into their associated IP addresses.

Dynamic Domain Name System (DDNS) DNS that supports dynamic updates of host name-to-IP address mappings.

Dynamic Host Configuration Protocol (DHCP) Service used to allocate IP addresses dynamically to network clients that are configured to obtain an address automatically.

Dynamic routing Method of routing used by routers to share their routing information on a network.

Dynamic updates Allow resources on a network to register with a zone and update any changes in their configurations dynamically.

Encapsulating Security Payload (ESP) Provides encryption, authentication, integrity, and anti-replay services.

Encrypting File System (EFS) A feature of Windows that allows users to encrypt files and folders that are stored on NTFS volumes through public key cryptography.

Enterprise CA A CA that is integrated with Active Directory and uses information stored there to identify users, computers, and services requesting certificates.

Event logging A feature that records remote access server warnings, errors, and other information in the system event log.

Event Viewer Maintains logs about program, security, and system events.

Exclusion An IP address that falls within the address range of a scope, but which the DHCP server may not lease to a client.

Exterior routing protocol A protocol, such as BGP (Border Gateway Protocol), used to exchange information between networks administered under different administrative authorities.

Filter Identifies the type of traffic that the filter action will be applied to. Filters include protocols, ports, IP addresses, DNS names.

Filter Action Identifies what to do if the filter matches.

Forward lookup zone A DNS zone that resolves host names to IP addresses.

Forwarder A DNS server outside of a firewall that can communicate with other DNS servers on the Internet enabling you to keep your internal DNS servers safe from harm behind the firewall.

Frame A logical grouping of information created at the Data link layer of the OSI model. It uses source/destination MAC addresses in the header.

Fully qualified domain name (FQDN) A method of naming a host using Internet naming conventions to fully identify the host, as in hostname.domain_name.

Globally Unique Identifier A unique number for the computer. It can be found in the BIOS, inside or outside of the computer case. Used by servers running the Remote Installation Service to control which clients it will service.

Group static mapping A type of static mapping used to create an entry for a group of computers.

Hop count The number of routers through which a data transmission must pass in order to reach its destination.

Host Any device on a network that is identified using an IP address.

Host ID The group of bits in the 32-bit IP address, distinct from the network bits and also known as the host address, that is used to identify individual network entities including servers, workstations, printers, routers, and gateways on a network.

Host name A name given to a host on a TCP/IP network in addition to the host's IP address.

Host name resolution A process, such as the TCP/IP utilities, DNS name resolution or WINS name resolution, that looks up the IP address of a host over a TCP/IP network by using a host name.

Hostname Utility used to display or set the host name of the local computer.

HOSTS file A text file available on the local computer that contains the static mappings of host names to IP addresses and is used by TCP/IP utilities to resolve host names to their IP addresses.

in-addr.arpa A special domain that contains nodes with names based on IP addresses to facilitate reverse lookups (finding a host name given an IP address).

in-addr.arpa zone The zone that is authoritative for the in-addr.arpa domain.

Infrared Data Association (IrDA) Protocol suite designed to provide line-of-sight wireless connectivity for devices such as a PDA or wireless mouse.

Instance Reflects how many occurrences of an object there are on the computer.

Integrity The process of ensuring that data received is accurate and complete.

Interior routing protocol A protocol, such as RIP (Routing Information Protocol), used to exchange routing information between routers administered under a common administrative authority.

Internet Assigned Numbers Authority (IANA) The organization that manages the root domain of the Internet. Web site: www.iana.org.

Internet Authentication Service (IAS) A service that enables you to configure a RADIUS server that can provide centralized remote authentication, authorization, and accounting capabilities for incoming connections instead of managing policies on individual servers.

Internet Control Message Protocol (ICMP) Protocol that supports packets containing error, control, and informational messages. The ping utility generates an ICMP Echo request.

Internet Group Management Protocol (IGMP) Protocol responsible for the management of IP multicasting, which is the transmission of an IP datagram to a set of hosts called the IP multicast group that is identified by a single IP multicast address.

Internet Key Exchange (IKE) A protocol that establishes the security associations between two entities.

Internet layer Layer in the DARPA model that is responsible for transferring packets between computers that are located on the same or different networks.

Internet Protocol (IP) A connectionless protocol that is responsible for the delivery of packets, including the process of fragmenting them and reassembling them at the destination.

Internet Protocol Security (IPSec) A suite of network-layer protocols that extends IP by providing authentication, confidentiality, and data integrity mechanisms for data in transit.

Internet Protocol version 4 (IPv4) The version of Internet Protocol that is generally installed by default during the installation of the Windows Server 2003 operating system.

Internet Protocol version 6 (IPv6) New version of Internet Protocol that has been developed to replace IPv4.

Intranet A private TCP/IP network within an organization.

IP Address Under IPv4, a 32-bit number divided into 4 octets separated by periods, used to identify a host on a TCP/IP network. An IP address has two parts: the network ID and the host ID. An IPv6 IP address has 128 bits.

IP Routing A technique that enables data transfer from one computer to another regardless of their physical locations or proximity.

IP Security Monitor A tool for testing whether IPSec communications are secure.

Ipconfig A command-line tool used to verify TCP/IP configuration settings.

IPSec Driver Uses the defined filters to determine which data packets are blocked, permitted, or secured.

IPSec Policy Agent (IPSec Services) Retrieves the appropriate IPSec policy and sends the information to the IPSec driver. The IPSec Policy Agent starts automatically at system startup. If no IPSec policies are assigned, it will wait for a policy to be assigned.

Iterative query A type of DNS query that calls a name server to reply with the data requested by a resolver or with a reference to another name server that would be able to answer the request of the resolver.

Jetpack A utility used to compact a WINS database.

Kerberos Used by IPSec for authentication.

Key Sequence of numbers created by an algorithm that is used to encrypt/decrypt information.

Layer Two Tunneling Protocol (L2TP) Protocol used to create a secure tunnel for virtual private networks.

LMHOSTS file A text file available on the local computer that contains the static mappings of NetBIOS names to IP addresses of computers and is used to resolve NetBIOS names to IP addresses.

Logical infrastructure Software components of a network including, but not limited to network protocols, IP addressing schemes, name resolution services, remote access services, routing, network address translation service, and security services.

Main Mode First phase of SA negotiation; involves authentication of entities.

Master name server See *Primary DNS server.*

Media Access Control Addresses Hardware addresses (48 bits) that are burned into network cards. They are used to uniquely identify the nodes on the network.

Member scopes The scopes included in a superscope.

Microsoft Certificate Services A service that enables Network Administrators to implement a Certificate Authority (CA) for issuing, renewing, managing, and revoking digital certificates.

Microsoft Challenge Handshake Authentication Protocol (MS-CHAP) v1 A protocol that encrypts password information before it is sent over a communication link, utilizing one-way authentication.

Microsoft Challenge Handshake Authentication Protocol (MS-CHAP) v2 An enhanced version of MS-CHAP v1 that utilizes mutual authentication.

Microsoft Management Console (MMC) A standard administrative interface for managing Windows Server 2003 and its applications.

Microsoft Point-to-Point Encryption A protocol used to secure remote access connections.

Modem Pool Consists of several modems integrated into a single card or several modems placed in an external chassis.

Multicast Address Dynamic Client Allocation Protocol (MADCAP) A standard introduced by the Internet Engineering Task Force (IETF) that defines the allocation of multicast addresses (see RFC 2730).

Multicast scope A group of Class D IP addresses that is used by a DHCP server to lease IP addresses to the multicast DHCP clients.

Multicasting The process of transmitting a message to a select group of recipients.

Mutual Authentication Authentication of both ends of a communication session.

Name query request A message sent by a WINS client to a WINS server requesting the IP address of a NetBIOS computer.

Name refresh request A message sent by a WINS client to a WINS server asking to refresh the TTL (Time-to-Live) of the NetBIOS name of the client.

Name registration request A message sent by a WINS client to a WINS server to register the NetBIOS name of the client.

Name release message A message sent by a WINS client to a WINS server when the client does not require the registered name any longer.

Name response message A message sent by a WINS server to a WINS client containing the IP address of the desired NetBIOS computer.

Name server A program that runs on a server computer that contains address information about network hosts.

Name server record A resource record that acts as a pointer to the name server of the delegated zone and directs the query to the correct name server for resolution.

NetBIOS An industry-standard interface between NetBIOS-based applications and TCP/IP protocols that is used for accessing NetBIOS services.

NetBIOS name A unique 16-byte name assigned to each NetBIOS resource on a network.

NetBIOS name cache A storage facility that stores information about recently resolved NetBIOS names.

NetBIOS name resolution The process of mapping a NetBIOS name to an IP address.

NetBIOS name server (NBNS) An application responsible for mapping NetBIOS names to IP addresses.

Netdiag Used to test the network driver, protocol driver, and the send and receive capabilities of your computer. It can also provide information on the IPSec policy that is currently active on the computer.

Netsh Command line utility that can be used to configure and monitor IPSec and perform DHCP and other administrative tasks from a command prompt.

Network access server Provides a dial-up or VPN entry point for remote access clients. Also known as a remote access server.

Network Address Translation (NAT) Routing protocol that exchanges information between routers and enables a LAN to use one set of IP addresses for internal traffic and another set of IP addresses for external traffic. NAT also allows multiple users to connect to the Internet through a single connection.

Network Bandwidth Bandwidth, measured in bits per second, is used to describe the amount of information that can be carried in a given amount of time. Also referred to as throughput.

Network ID The group of bits in an IP address also known as the network address that identify the network to which a computer belongs, as opposed to the Host ID bits, which identify the computer itself.

Network infrastructure Interconnected computers and the services required for communication between the computers.

Network Interface layer Layer in the DARPA model that is responsible for sending and receiving TCP/IP packets (and those of many other protocols) over network media.

Network Monitor Tool for capturing and monitoring packets.

NWLink Microsoft's 32-bit implementation of Novell NetWare's IPX/SPX protocol.

Object Represents any system component that can be measured.

Octet Any of the four 8-bit values used in an IP address.

Offline compaction A WINS server database process that you need to perform, after stopping the WINS service, to reduce the amount of disk space used by scavenged entries.

One-way authentication Authentication of only one end of the communication session. Typically the client is authenticated by the server.

Online compaction An automatic WINS server database compaction process that occurs in the background during idle time.

Open Shortest Path First (OSPF) Routing protocol that enables routers to exchange routing table information so that routers can find optimal routes for data transfer.

Open Systems Interconnection Model This 7-layer model serves as a reference for how messages are transmitted between two network devices.

Packet An individual unit in a communications stream, also known as a frame, datagram, or message depending on the context in which it is used.

Parsing The process that Network Monitor uses to read, analyze, and describe the contents of a frame.

Pathping Utility that combines the features of ping and tracert.

Performance Logs and Alerts A tool that allows an Administrator to capture data over an extended period of time for later review and analysis.

Physical infrastructure Hardware components of a network, including cables, network interface cards, hubs, and routers.

Ping (Packet Internet Groper) Used to test connectivity in IP-based networks.

Pointer (PTR) record A resource record in the reverse lookup file that associates an IP address with a host name in the in-addr.arpa domain.

Point-to-Point Protocol An industry standard protocol that is used to transport multiprotocol datagrams over point-to-point links. PPP is documented in RFC 1661.

Point-to-Point Tunneling Protocol (PPTP) TCP/IP protocol that provides an internal address configuration to the remote client; used in virtual private networks.

Positive name registration response A message sent by a WINS server to a WINS client indicating successful registration of the NetBIOS name of the client in the WINS database.

Pragmatic General Multicast (PGM) The reliable multicast protocol supported by Windows Server 2003 to transmit messages in a multicast data stream.

Pre-shared Key Used in IPSec communications for authentication.

Primary DNS server/Primary name server The name server that gets data for its zones from locally stored zone database files and is the main authority for its zones.

Promiscuous Mode Network interface cards operating in this mode accept all traffic regardless of the MAC address in the packet.

Protocol Predefined set of rules for sending information over a network. A protocol standardizes the content, format, timing, sequencing, and manner of error control of messages that are transmitted between devices on a network.

Protocol Analyzer A device that captures network traffic for analysis.

Public Key Infrastructure A set of services that supports the use of cryptography. Includes rules, policies, standards, and software that manage certificates and public/private keys in order to authenticate the validity of each party involved in a transaction.

Public/private keys Key pairs used to encrypt/decrypt information and verify digital signatures.

Pull partner A WINS server that pulls or requests replication of updated WINS database entries from other WINS servers at a configured interval.

Push partner A WINS server that notifies other WINS servers of the need to replicate their database entries at a configured interval.

Quick Mode Second phase of SA negotiations when security protocols are negotiated.

RADIUS client A remote access server to which remote clients can connect. RADIUS clients are configured to send requests to a RADIUS server running IAS.

RADIUS proxy A capability available through IAS that forwards authentication and accounting requests to other RADIUS servers.

RADIUS server With IAS installed, a RADIUS server can provide centralized remote authentication, authorization, and accounting capabilities for incoming connections.

Recovery Agent A person who has a public key certificate for the purpose of recovering user data that has been encrypted when EFS is implemented.

Recursive query A type of DNS query that calls a name server that assumes the full workload and responsibility for providing a complete answer to the query.

Remote Authentication Dial-In Service (RADIUS) A security authentication protocol used to authenticate and authorize dial-up and VPN connection users.

Remote Installation Service Used to provide images on demand for operating system installations.

Replay Attack An attack that is based on capturing packets and then resending them on the network.

Reservation Permits you to set aside a specific address in a scope for leasing by a particular DHCP client.

Resolver A host service that provides information about other network hosts to the client. The resolver initiates the search for an IP address once it is provided with the host name.

Resource record An entry in a DNS database that contains information about the resources in a DNS domain. Examples of resource records include name server (NS), start of authority (SOA), and alias (CNAME).

Resultant Set of Policy (RSoP) snap-in Tool used to simulate and test policy settings that are applied to computers or users using Group Policy.

Reverse lookup file A zone database file containing information that allows for finding a host name, given the IP address of the host.

Reverse lookup zone A zone that resolves IP addresses to host names.

RFC Refers to Request for Comments, the main technical documentation series maintained by the Internet Engineering Task Force

RIPv1 Distance vector routing protocol that provides information about the networks to which a router can connect and the distances to these networks.

RIPv2 Routing protocol that is an enhanced version of RIPv1 and provides the information about the subnet mask and broadcasts the routing information.

Root Certification Authority The most trusted CA in the PKI. It is at the top of the CA hierarchy and signs its own digital certificate. There is no higher level of certifying authority in the hierarchy. Typically used to issue certificates to subordinate CAs.

Root domain The domain at the top of the DNS namespace hierarchy.

Root name server The DNS server that has authority for the top-most domain in the DNS hierarchy.

Root zone The zone authoritative for the root domain.

Route Command used to modify the local routing table.

Router A network device used to transfer data between networks. You can use a router to connect LANs, as well as connecting a LAN to a WAN or to the Internet.

Routes Entries in a routing table that define the path to a network based on its IP address.

Routing The process of selecting the path by which a source computer transfers packets of data across networks to a destination computer.

Routing and Remote Access Service (RRAS) Multiprotocol routing service that enables routing of data traffic on IP, IPX, and AppleTalk networks, as well as providing remote access capabilities. You use RRAS to connect remote clients working from remote locations to a network.

Routing Information Protocol (RIP) Enables a router to exchange routing information with other routers to update them about changes in the network topology.

Routing table Table containing information records about networks and gateways known to the local host, including the host's own network. A routing table also specifies which gateway is to be used to forward packets to specific non-local networks.

Scope A pool of IP addresses and other related configuration parameters from which a DHCP server offers leases to its clients.

Secedit Command line equivalent of the Security Configuration and Analysis tool.

Secondary DNS server/Secondary name server A name server that contains a copy of the zone database file downloaded from the primary DNS server of a zone.

Second-level domain The level of domains under the top-level domains in the DNS namespace hierarchy.

Secret key cryptography A method of hiding information in transit that involves sharing a private or secret key between the two individuals involved in a communication session. Secret key cryptography is also known as symmetric cryptography.

Secure Server (Require Security) A default IPSec policy under which a computer will accept communications only if they are IPSec-enabled. The policy can be used on servers or clients.

Security Association Defines the encryption and authentication protocols used in the session.

Security Configuration and Analysis Tool used to analyze security settings and apply security templates.

Security template Allows administrators to set a wide range of security settings on computers.

Security Template snap-in Tool used to create and modify security template files.

Server (Request Security) A default IPSec policy that is assigned to servers or clients that will be involved in communications with both Windows Server 2003 computers and computers running down-level operating systems.

Services Programs that are started when the computer boots and, in some cases, continue to run in the background.

Spoofing Forging the source IP address of packets' addresses so it will appear as if they originated from a trusted host.

Standalone CA A CA that is not integrated with Active Directory. If Active Directory does exist, it can interact with a Standalone CA.

Standard primary zone A zone that stores DNS information in a text file.

Standard secondary zone A zone that maintains a read-only copy of the zone database, which is downloaded from the primary name server.

Start of Authority (SOA) The zone record that declares a server as authoritative for the zone and includes attributes such as the zone server name, contact name, refresh interval TTL values, and more.

Static mapping entry A non-dynamic name resolution entry in a WINS database.

Static routing Refers to hosts obtaining their data packet transmission paths using a manually built routing table.

Stub zone An abridged copy of a zone whose purpose is simply to maintain name server (NS) records for the name servers that resolve requests that are made in the master zone.

Sub-domain The level of domains under the second-level domains in the DNS namespace hierarchy.

Subnet mask 32-bit value that is used to distinguish the network ID and the host ID in an IP address. The network mask (or customized subnet mask) is used to make routing decisions. It distinguishes which bits of the 32-bit IP address are network bits: the "one-bits" in the subnet mask identify which of the 32 bits are network bits, and the "zero-bits" identify the host bits.

Subnetting Breaking a large network down into smaller, more manageable pieces.

Subordinate Certification Authority A CA that receives its certificate from a parent CA. Subordinate CAs provide certificates to users/computers/services on a network.

Superscopes Used to group and manage multiple scopes from one DHCP server.

System log A component of the Events Viewer that logs system events; enables you to obtain detailed information about related events that are recorded during DHCP audit logging.

System Monitor A tool that provides real-time monitoring that can provide you with valuable insight as to how processes are progressing using the process, memory, and disk input/output on the server.

Systems Management Server Provides application deployment, asset management, and monitoring services.

Task Manager A tool that provides information regarding the processes and programs that are running on the computer. Task Manager provides a quick method for monitoring memory and processor utilization as well.

TCP/IP filtering Method used to control the type of traffic that can enter a network based on port numbers.

Time-to-Live (TTL) The period of time for which information can be considered valid before it should be discarded.

Top-level domain The level of domains under the root domain in the DNS namespace hierarchy. Examples of top-level domains are .com, .net, .org, .ca, .uk, .au, and .biz.

Trace logs A tool that is used to collect information on memory events, such as a page fault, or resource events, such as disk input/output.

Tracert Utility used to search the route taken when data is transferred between communicating devices and to discover the point at which communication has failed. It displays the Fully Qualified Domain Name and IP address of each gateway along the route to a remote host.

Transmission Control Protocol (TCP) A network protocol that provides a one-to-one, stream-oriented, and reliable delivery of data between computers.

Transmission Control Protocol/Internet Protocol (TCP/IP) Protocol suite that enables computers to communicate with each other across a network. TCP/IP is the core set of protocols used by the Internet; can be used on both large and small networks to transfer data between computers using different operating systems and widely varying hardware platforms.

Transport layer Layer in the DARPA model that is responsible for establishing a connection between communicating devices and for transferring data.

Transport Mode The default mode for IPSec that protects the data over the entire path between two computers.

Tunnel Mode Under IPSec, a mode that protects data between two endpoints (typically routers/gateways). Traffic behind the routers/gateways remains unencrypted.

Unicast A packet that is sent to a specific computer.

Unique static mapping A static mapping type used to create a static mapping entry for each IP address.

User Datagram Protocol (UDP) Protocol that provides a one-to-one or one-to-many connectionless communications service. UDP is unreliable, as it does not guarantee the delivery of data.

Variable Length Subnet Masking (VLSM) A method of changing subnetting by removing the requirement that all subnets be of equal size. VLSM allows you to break an IP address up into its largest subnets and then subnet the subnets.

Virtual Private Network (VPN) A virtual network that can provide a secure connection between a user on an external network, such as the Internet, and an internal corporate network.

Virtual Private Network (VPN) tunnel A secure tunnel between two or more devices across a public network. Encryption and authentication protocols protect the data while in transit.

Windows Internet Name Service (WINS) Microsoft's implementation of a NetBIOS name server; used to translate NetBIOS names to IP addresses in order to locate a computer on a network.

WINS client A computer on the network that has been assigned the address of a WINS server to use for NetBIOS name resolutions.

WINS database The database used by WINS to resolve NetBIOS names to IP addresses.

WINS proxy agent A WINS client that allows non-WINS clients to participate in network communications.

WINS replication The method of sharing information among WINS servers on a network.

WINS server A server program that runs WINS for the purpose of resolving NetBIOS names to IP addresses.

X.509 certificate standards Standards that define the format and contents of a digital certificate. RFC 3647 discusses this standard in detail.

Zone An administrative unit of DNS that is responsible for a portion of the DNS namespace; contains information about domains within that portion.

Zone database file The database on a DNS server that contains information about a zone.

Zone delegation The process of dividing a large single zone into smaller zones, which are responsible for managing a portion of the DNS namespace for which the original zone was responsible.

Zone of authority The part of the DNS namespace for which a zone is responsible.

Zone transfer The process of transferring changes in the zone database file from the primary DNS server to the secondary DNS server.

Exam 70-291 Objectives

IMPLEMENTING, MANAGING, AND MAINTAINING IP ADDRESSING

1.01 Configure TCP/IP addressing on a server computer.

1.02 Manage DHCP.
- 1.02 (a) Manage DHCP clients and leases.
- 1.02 (b) Manage DHCP Relay Agent.
- 1.02 (c) Manage DHCP databases.
- 1.02 (d) Manage DHCP scope options.
- 1.02 (e) Manage reservations and reserved clients.

1.03 Troubleshoot TCP/IP addressing.
- 1.03 (a) Diagnose and resolve issues related to Automatic Private IP Addressing (APIPA).
- 1.03 (b) Diagnose and resolve issues related to incorrect TCP/IP configuration.

1.04 Troubleshoot DHCP.
- 1.04 (a) Diagnose and resolve issues related to DHCP authorization.
- 1.04 (b) Verify DHCP reservation configuration.
- 1.04 (c) Examine the system event log and DHCP server audit log files to find related events.
- 1.04 (d) Diagnose and resolve issues related to configuration of DHCP server and scope options.
- 1.04 (e) Verify that the DHCP Relay Agent is working correctly.
- 1.04 (f) Verify database integrity.

IMPLEMENTING, MANAGING, AND MAINTAINING NAME RESOLUTION

2.01 Install and configure the DNS Server service.
- 2.01 (a) Configure DNS server options.
- 2.01 (b) Configure DNS zone options.
- 2.01 (c) Configure DNS forwarding.

2.02 Manage DNS.
- 2.02 (a) Manage DNS zone settings.
- 2.02 (b) Manage DNS record settings.
- 2.02 (c) Manage DNS server options.

2.03 Monitor DNS. Tools might include System Monitor, Event Viewer, Replication Monitor, and DNS debug logs.

IMPLEMENTING, MANAGING, AND MAINTAINING NETWORK SECURITY

3.01 Implement secure network administration procedures.
- 3.01 (a) Implement security baseline settings and audit security settings by using security templates.
- 3.01 (b) Implement the principle of least privilege.

3.02 Monitor network protocol security. Tools might include the IP Security Monitor Microsoft Management Console (MMC) snap-in and Kerberos support tools.

3.03 Troubleshoot network protocol security. Tools might include the IP Security Monitor MMC snap-in, Event Viewer, and Network Monitor.

IMPLEMENTING, MANAGING, AND MAINTAINING ROUTING AND REMOTE ACCESS

4.01 Configure Routing and Remote Access user authentication.
- 4.01 (a) Configure remote access authentication protocols.
- 4.01 (b) Configure Internet Authentication Service (IAS) to provide authentication for Routing and Remote Access clients.
- 4.01 (c) Configure Routing and Remote Access policies to permit or deny access.

4.02 Manage remote access.
- 4.02 (a) Manage packet filters.
- 4.02 (b) Manage Routing and Remote Access routing interfaces.
- 4.02 (c) Manage devices and ports.
- 4.02 (d) Manage routing protocols.
- 4.02 (e) Manage Routing and Remote Access clients.

Exam 70-291 Objectives (cont'd)

4.03 Manage TCP/IP routing.
- 4.03 (a) Manage routing protocols.
- 4.03 (b) Manage routing tables.
- 4.03 (c) Manage routing ports.

4.04 Implement secure access between private networks.

4.05 Troubleshoot user access to remote access services.
- 4.05 (a) Diagnose and resolve issues related to remote access VPNs.
- 4.05 (b) Diagnose and resolve issues related to establishing a remote access connection.
- 4.05 (c) Diagnose and resolve user access to resources beyond the remote access server.

4.06 Troubleshoot Routing and Remote Access routing.
- 4.06 (a) Troubleshoot demand-dial routing.
- 4.06 (b) Troubleshoot router-to-router VPNs.

MAINTAINING A NETWORK INFRASTRUCTURE

5.01 Monitor network traffic. Tools might include Network Monitor and System Monitor.

5.02 Troubleshoot connectivity to the Internet.

5.03 Troubleshoot server services.
- 5.03 (a) Diagnose and resolve issues related to service dependency.
- 5.03 (b) Use server recovery options to diagnose and resolve service-related issues.

NOTES

NOTES

NOTES

NOTES

NOTES

NOTES

NOTES

NOTES